Praise for

GOD'S PRESENCE IN YOUR FUNDRAISING

"I have wanted Scott to write this book for years. There is nothing
like it anywhere! Those of us who raise funds sometimes get discouraged and lose heart. In every chapter, Scott takes us back to
the Scriptures to restore our vision and purpose. Meditate daily on
these devotionals and discover a whole new joy and perspective in
your fundraising."

—**Steve Shadrach**, Global Ambassador, Center for
Mission Mobilization

"Scott Morton has personally helped hundreds of Christian leaders and mission workers come to a deeper understanding of fundraising and its critical role in Christ's mission. He knows well the
fears that leaders face and seeks to help them find the freedom and
joy they need to be successful in their fundraising efforts.

"This is not a 'how-to' book, but rather a call to see fundraising
as a biblical part of Christian ministry. Through meditation on the
Scriptures, prayer, and a closer daily walk with Christ, you can be
strengthened for the task of raising the necessary funding for the
mission of Christ in the world today."

—**John Stevens**, Pastor Emeritus, First Presbyterian Church,
Colorado Springs

"Short and to the point, these 40 chapters capture biblical insights
and prayers Scott has discovered during many years of living on
gift-income. Be inspired to be brought back to God as the source
of your lifestyle as a gospel worker."

—**Leendert de Jong**, Agape Trainer, Ministr.
Development, Amsterdam, H

"Such great encouragement ... Th
the lessons are deep and thought
sages are spot-on, and the prayers   .. look forward to
using this devotional to spur me on in my fundraising journey."

—**Carol Njuguna**, Navigators, Staff Development and Care,
Nairobi, Kenya

"When I started recruiting resources for Christian ministries, both personally and corporately, I spent a year in the Bible deciding if God thought it was legitimate. Along with the Bible and my friend Scott Morton, I received spiritual freedom to be excited about recruiting people to eternal causes.

"Scott Morton has a God-given passion to help people experience the joy and freedom of the vision God has planted in their hearts. Scott's practical and heartwarming stories entwined with Bible verses reassure fundraisers of God's intervention in their work."

—**Lauren Libby**, International President/CEO, TWR International

"My long time friend and mentor, Scott Morton, uses his humility and witty insights, grounded in Scripture, to remind us never to take our eyes off Jesus. Regardless of where you are in the journey of fundraising, this book will help you remain rooted in the most important thing: Jesus Christ!"

—**Ken Chi**, Navigators Collegiate National Leadership Team, Ethnic & International Funding Trainer and Coach

"If I were to title Scott Morton's latest help for support-raising gospel workers, it would be Daily Vitamins for Support Raisers. Scott has hit another home run with this book. I like the guideline that 'fundraising is God's idea, just like my call to ministry.' I can't wait to put this vital resource into the hands of every gospel worker in Africa."

—**Emeka & Bilhatu Ohahuru**, International Fundraising Coach, The Navigators, Lagos, Nigeria.

"Scott Morton is both a student and teacher of the scriptures. Let *God's Presence in Your Fundraising* reach into your life. You will grow deeper in your own walk with the Father and be better positioned to mobilize others in advancing God's kingdom."

—**Mike Riggins**, Team Lead, North American Mission Board, SBC

"*God's Presence in Your Fundraising* will bring you back to the Bible as your drawing board, away from your opinions on fundraising. Scott draws out familiar readings of Scripture to shed new light on the connection between the gospel and fundraising.

"I pray that reading this book will move you from discouragement to excitement in fundraising and that you will not overlook the unprecedented work of God who has gone before you. Let us come to Him daily!"

— **Mary Kaigai-Odhiambo**, The Navigators, Fundraising
   Coach, Kenya

"In *God's Presence in Your Fundraising*, Scott Morton helps bridge the sacred-secular divide that we face as fundraisers and fundraising coaches. He helps us focus on the Bible through down-to-earth, relatable stories and meditations and prayers that address our hearts. I pray that you too will be refreshed as you read this book."

— **Naftali Odhiambo Oswago**, The Navigators, Fundraising
   Coach, Kenya

"Scott Morton goes deep inside the fundraiser's heart to address the hidden but most destructive obstacles. This book will be a precious companion to those who raise funds for the glory of God!"

— **Serge Sess**, The Navigators, Country Director, Côte d'Ivoire

"In the midst of our busy fundraising activities and implementing best practices, *God's Presence in Your Fundraising* points us back to the Word of God as our foundation. Scott's examples from Scripture, his years of ministry and fundraising experience, and his practical insights connect us more deeply to Christ as we develop ministry partners."

— **Molly Gilberts**, Ministry Partner Development
   Communications, The Navigators, U.S.

"Scott Morton knows fundraising. Whenever my clients are looking for help in fundraising that is in line with their Christian faith, I direct them to Scott's books and trainings. I know he will show them strategies grounded in Scripture and built on experience that will help them get their ministry fully funded."

—**Marc Pitman**, Concord Leadership Group

"In *God's Presence in Your Fundraising*, Scott Morton gifts us a treasure trove from God's word. It builds a foundation for our funding plans and offers an antidote to our discouragements and fears. Dive into it, immerse yourself in the biblical truths in every chapter, then head out with confidence and excitement to discover whom God has already called to partner with you in his gospel harvest."

—**Myles Wilson**, Founder, Funding the Family Business, United Kingdom

"This devotional will anchor you deeper in the biblical perspective of what it means to raise support. *God's Presence in Your Fundraising* contains reflective and practical guidance on how to stay grounded in Jesus during the highs and lows of support raising. What a vital resource!"

—**Jenn Fortner**, Financial Partnership Development, Assemblies of God World Missions

God's Presence in Your Fundraising

40 Prayers & Readings

40

READINGS & PRAYERS

GOD'S PRESENCE

IN

YOUR FUNDRAISING

Scott Morton

CMM Center for Mission Mobilization

ISBN: 978-1-947468-61-0

Published by Center for Mission Mobilization
PO Box 3556
Fayetteville, AR 72702
For more resources, visit mobilization.org/resources

All Scripture references taken from New American Standard Bible (NASB) Copyright © 1960, 1962, 1963, 1968, 1971, 1972, 1973, 1975, 1977, 1995 by The
Lockman Foundation. Used by permission. All rights reserved.

All Greek words referenced by the author are from *An Expository Dictionary of New
Testament Words: With Their Precise Meanings for English Readers* by William Edwy Vine,
Fleming H. Revell Company, New Jersey, 1966.

Map research by Katie Moum.

Translations
We desire to make this material available to as many as will use it around the
world in a way that honors everyone involved in the work. If you would like to
translate or adapt this resource to use in your cultural context, please contact us.
There are guidelines for translators at mobilization.org/translation.

Printed in the United States of America

First Edition, First Imprint, 2021.
C: 09-08-21   M: 09-24-21 16:13

presented to

---

from

---

dated

TABLE OF CONTENTS

I first met Scott Morton in the year 2000 when he graciously allowed me to attend his Navigator staff support raising training. Little did I know he would become such an influential mentor in my life and ministry in the decades to come. I had never met anyone so committed to studying, modeling, and teaching the biblical principles of money, giving, and funding ministry. I once asked Scott to evaluate the support raising boot camp training curriculum I had created. When we reconvened a month later, I was certain he would be impressed, but after observing he had marked up every single page, he announced, "I'd give it about a 'C'." After a long, but effective pause, he slyly smiled and added, "but I can tell you how to make it an 'A'." And he did!

Now, it's your turn. If you're feeling like your support raising perspective, confidence, preparation, or faith deserves a less-than-stellar grade, *God's Presence in Your Fundraising* is for you. I've been after Scott for years to produce these biblically-based, spiritually-nourishing, conviction-building daily devotionals to guide and encourage ministry support raisers everywhere. And he did!

Lastly, I can tell you Scott is no theorist. For over 50 years he has sought to live a spirit-filled and directed life, depending upon God and His Word, constantly seeking to recruit people, and their resources, to the person and purposes of Jesus Christ. Why, you might ask? Well, to quote Scott, "It's all about the gospel."

Enjoy!

—Steve Shadrach
Global Ambassador, Center for Mission Mobilization

My own fundraising journey began with frustration. Besides a myriad of how-to questions, my conscience bothered me:

* Is fundraising secular or truly biblical?
* Why do I feel guilty about asking for money?
* Why doesn't God automatically provide so I can get on with ministry?
* Will I offend friends if I appeal to them?
* Others seem to raise support with ease, but what about me? Will God do miracles on my behalf?

Traditional fundraising tactics did not address these deep questions nor my angst about asking. I needed answers that spoke to my heart. But there was no time to casually ponder. With only a handful of donors, we couldn't pay our bills.

It was then that my wife graciously asked, "Are you going to support this family or not?" Her question was from Heaven, and it nudged me to ransack the Bible for answers. I looked in the concordance under "fundraising" and found nothing. But, by God's grace, one by one, passages of Scripture came tumbling toward me that directly answered my conscience questions. Financial freedom followed.

Year by year, the Bible remains my go-to source for guidance, whether in raising personal support, planning for major donor funding, ministering to giving partners, or mentoring others.

That's my story about the importance of the Bible! I'm eager to hear yours.

No matter where you are in your fundraising journey, I pray the Bible speaks to you deeply as your day-by-day fundraising guide.

Father in Heaven,

I pray today for the readers of this book — my gospel-advancing friends!

I pray You will draw near to them during their fundraising adventures as they phone and text a dozen times to secure an appointment, nervously meet with prospective partners, and minister to those from all walks of life.

May these 40 devotionals come alive as they submit their opinions about money to You.

Even now, prepare the hearts of those to whom they will make appeals. Give my readers passion as they share their spiritual journey to Christ and as they explain their ministry calling. Ease their sweaty palms. Help them to listen genuinely, ask boldly, and treat each prospective giving partner with respect, no matter what they decide. May they experience Your Presence in each appointment.

I ask also that their funding journey takes them to those who need Christ — friends, family, acquaintances, or strangers. Through their funding appointments, may skeptics meet You for the first time and may believers know You better. We boldly ask You for miracles!

Father of the cattle on a thousand hills, help my readers understand that there are no cash flow problems in Heaven. May they see You as the God of Ephesians 3:20, "able to do far more abundantly beyond all we ask or think."

In all their funding activities, may Your Name be honored.

Through Christ, Amen.

From my heart to yours,

Scott Morton

Scott Morton

1

SEVEN FINANCIAL WORDS TO PRAY DAILY

Give us this day our daily bread.

MATTHEW 6:11

Early in my ministry, I was lamenting to my colleague, Duane, that we were struggling financially. He listened patiently, then asked, "Do you pray about your finances? Do your pray about your finances *every day?*"

I replied weakly, "Not *every* day."

Duane quickly exhorted, "If I were you, I'd pray about it *every day!*"

Good advice. A few months later in my Bible reading, I came to the Lord's Prayer, "Give us this day our daily bread," and Duane's advice was sealed in my heart.

The Lord's prayer contains six requests. The first three are about God and His Kingdom, and the keyword is *your*:

1 May *your* name be hallowed.
2 May *your* kingdom come.
3 May *your* will be done.

The second three requests are about the people on earth, and the keyword is *us*:

4 Give *us* our daily bread.
5 Forgive *us* our debts.
6 Lead *us* not into temptation (including deliver *us* from evil).

Requests #1–3 are theological, #5 is relational, and #6 is moral — lofty spiritual longings. But #4 is unabashedly down-to-earth. Jesus, the Son of God, the most spiritual man who ever lived, prayed about physical food!

Two chapters earlier on the Mount of Temptation, Jesus told the devil, "Man shall *not* live on bread alone, but on every word that proceeds from the mouth of God" (Matthew 4:4). Throughout history, super-spiritual ascetics lived meagerly, starving themselves to achieve holiness. They concluded that bread was not important. But Jesus did not say, "Man shall not live on bread *at all*."

Gospel worker, you are spiritually minded, called to teach in the Heavenly realm, but don't neglect the physical realm. Though you are "fearfully and wonderfully made," (Psalm 139:14) you still need bread!

Remember, though, we pray for *daily bread*, not *daily cake,* as humorously expressed by author, Dale Bruner, in *Matthew, a Commentary.*

It's also *daily bread*, not a *10-year supply of bread*. It's only for today. As we pray for bread "this day," we acknowledge our dependence on the Lord "this day" and every day. That's why I bring my monthly budget — the exact amount — to the Lord every day in prayer.

Note also that the Lord's prayer is corporate — *our* daily bread, not *my* daily bread. Besides ourselves, let us ask for those without bread. The word "our" reminds us to think about others.

Finally, this prayer is addressed to our Father in Heaven — our true source. Jesus lifts our eyes to the skies — beyond giving partners, beyond savings accounts, beyond a guaranteed paycheck. All these could blow away like dandelion fluff in a summer wind.

A missionary was talking to a friend outside their church one Sunday morning. The friend asked the missionary if he raised personal support or if he was paid through the general fund of his agency. The missionary replied piously, "I trust God for my income." The friend paused a moment, then said, "I own a printing company with three employees, and I too trust God for my income." What a powerful reminder that we are not the only ones trusting God for our income!

"Give us this day our daily bread." Let us not trust in our communication skill, our dazzling vision, or our mailing list. Let us *daily* ask our faithful Father for bread. He is the source.

"Back of the bread is the snowy flour; And back of the flour the mill. And back of the mill is the wheat and the shower, And the sun and the Father's will."

—*MALTBIE D. BABCOCK, AMERICAN CLERGYMAN (1858–1901)*

PRAYER

*Father in Heaven, I confess I neglect to look to You **every day** as my source. But now I ask You anew for daily bread. And please show me how to assist others in my world who are without bread. Amen.*

2

ARE YOU COUNTING ON THE PRECEDING WORK OF GOD?

The next day [John the Baptist] saw Jesus coming to him and said, "Behold, the Lamb of God who takes away the sin of the world!"

JOHN 1:29

Our passage today has nothing to do with fundraising, and yet it has everything to do with fundraising. Especially when you feel alone.

At a place called Bethany, east of the Jordan River, John the Baptist *saw Jesus coming to him.* John was not moving toward Jesus — Jesus was moving toward John. This is a physical example of a grand theological truth. Throughout

Scripture, before people move toward God, He moves toward them. I call it *the preceding work of God*.

Romans 5:8b says, "While we were yet sinners, Christ died for us." He didn't die for us because we were seeking Him. He moved toward us first. "We love because He first loved us" (1 John 4:19).

In your fundraising appeals, it is important to share your spiritual history. Can you remember the details of how Jesus moved toward you? Perhaps my story will spur your memory.

In the basement of our country church in Iowa hung a painting of Jesus knocking at the door. I pondered that painting every Sunday. As a five-year-old Presbyterian, I thought religion was for old people. Still, I couldn't get that picture out of my mind.

Upon high school graduation, a neighbor gave me a pocket devotional with Scriptures, poems, and prayers. I took it with me to my university but hardly glanced at it. I was drifting from God, doing things I knew were wrong. But I consoled myself that I was more righteous than my buddies on the baseball team.

One Saturday afternoon, a grad student came to my dorm room and asked to talk about spiritual things. I happily agreed, thinking I could help him. He drew a bridge diagram about eternal life, and shared Ephesians 2:8–9: "By grace you have been saved," but I didn't like the notion of being saved by grace and not by good deeds.

Christ moved toward me again during a Christian meeting when a businessman from Kansas City quoted Revelation 3:20, "Behold, I stand at the door and knock." My mind flashed back to that church basement painting. Convicted about my prideful self-righteousness, I went into a chapel that very afternoon and confessed my sinful ways. Visualizing the painting, I opened the door to Christ.

Then what? Shouldn't I feel different? No angel feathers wafted down from Heaven. Was it real?

Two days later, back on campus, I was telling a dirty story to some buddies. Halfway through the story, feelings of uncleanliness washed over me. I was stunned. "Guys," I said, "I can't finish this story." And I walked away. Christ had become personal.

How about you? Can you trace how Christ moved toward you — how He became real to you? Don't say your spiritual journey is boring! It might be unspectacular, but God's work is not boring! Your listeners might identify with your story and move toward Christ.

When you go for a funding appointment, you are not alone. God has already moved toward you and toward those you are meeting. Do not overlook the "preceding work of God."

At your appointment, tell about how God's preceding work in your life drew you to Christ. And ask your friend to share his or her spiritual journey too. Lifelong bonds are formed with these meaningful conversations.

In your fundraising, are you counting on the preceding work of God?

PRAYER

Father in Heaven, thank you for taking initiative to move toward me even though I often ignored You. Today I take courage knowing that You are also moving toward potential giving partners like _____ and_____. Amen.

3

ASK — A PROMISE AWAITS

Ask, and it will be given to you; seek, and you will find;
knock, and it will be opened to you.

MATTHEW 7:7

Ugandan gospel worker, "Henry," told me a God-story about
asking. He wanted to attend the Safari 6 Ministry Equipping
Conference in America but did not have $2,000 for airfare.
His wife saw how badly Henry wanted to go and encouraged
him not to give up. In Henry's words...

As I sat and pondered the large sum of money I needed for
the plane ticket, I noticed a book on my shelf that should have
been returned to a friend a year earlier. Embarrassed, not
knowing if he was even in town, I decided to drop everything
and bring the book to his office.

He picked up my call, and straightway I went to his office.

During our catch-up visit, I discovered my friend traveled much for business. Taking a risk, I asked if he ever shared his frequent flyer miles with others. "Sometimes, but KLM only," he said.

So, I mentioned the Safari 6 Conference and how it would benefit me and my ministry, then I swallowed hard and asked if he would consider giving flyer miles for my trip.

My friend said, "The KLM Office is across the street. Here's my frequent flyer code — go get yourself a ticket!"

Within two hours, Henry went from being despondent about getting to Safari 6 to walking into his home and joyfully showing his prayerful wife a round-trip airplane ticket!

What happened here? Most importantly, Henry was surrendered to God's leading about attending the conference. God knew his heart's desire, Henry and his wife here praying about it, and in God's providence, Henry noticed a long overdue book in his bookcase. Henry's willingness to ask his friend to consider giving a plane ticket led to an amazing act of generosity. He did not scheme nor hint! He made a bold, honest ministry appeal to a friend.

In our passage today, Jesus invites you to *ask, seek, and knock*...without conditions. Imagine Jesus calling to you from the mercy seat in Heaven, *Come on, don't be shy. Ask Me for something!*

Following today's text, Jesus said if a child asked his earthly father for bread, will he give him a stone? If he asked his father for a fish, would he give him a snake? Matthew 7:11 concludes, "Your Father who is in Heaven will give what is good to those who ask Him."

Our Father will answer your prayer in His way and give you what is good according to His eternal wisdom, not according to your smallish or sometimes selfish desires. This promise is the guardrail of your prayer life.

My friend, for what are you asking the Father? What are

you seeking? For what are you knocking? Is your goal to "get by" or to achieve 100 percent of your budget?

Thou art coming to a King,
Large petitions with thee bring;
For his grace and power are such,
None can ever ask too much.

— *JOHN NEWTON, CONVERTED SLAVE-TRADER (1725–1807)*

First step? Check your bookcase or any other subtle nudge from the Holy Spirit!

Second, who needs to hear your ministry vision in the next six weeks?

PRAYER

*Father in Heaven, I do not think of you as **longing** for me to ask. So now, I ask you for full funding. And for boldness to invite friends and acquaintances to join my ministry. I am asking them, but I am actually asking **you**! I trust you as I ask, seek, and knock. Amen.*

OUTSIDE YOUR
COMFORT ZONE?

*Arise, go to Zarephath, which belongs to Sidon, and stay
there; behold, I have commanded a widow there to provide
for you.*

1 KINGS 17:9

Asking someone to go outside their comfort zone is considered bad manners, crossing a line, and downright rude. But our Father in Heaven operates differently. In today's text, God commanded the prophet Elijah to leave his comfort zone to touch a poor widow's life. This created an uncomfortable change for Elijah.

Do you know the story?

On the run from wicked Queen Jezebel, God commanded Elijah to hide by Cherith Brook, east of the Jordan. Miraculously, ravens brought Elijah food each day, and he drank from the brook; this was God's provision during a time of waiting. It was not a balanced diet, but okay for a prophet in hiding!

Day 4

1 Kings 17:9

However, under God's sovereignty, Cherith Brook dried up. God then commanded Elijah to seek out a widow in Zarephath of Sidon, the hometown of Jezebel. We can imagine Elijah asking, "Really? Sidon? The pagan land of Jezebel who is trying to kill me?"

Jezabel's Sidonians were prosperous. They marketed a valuable purple dye from the shell of the Murex clam found in their coastal waters. And they worshiped Baal (the storm god) and his consort Astarte (the god of fertility). Queen Jezebel brought to the Jewish nation the Sidonian practice of child sacrifice as well as sexual promiscuity. Elijah had spoken against these depraved religious practices and was now on Jezebel's hit list.

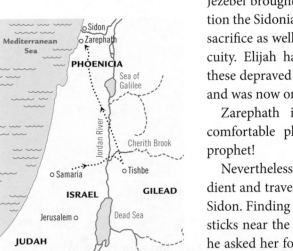

Zarephath in Sidon — not a comfortable place for a Jewish prophet!

Nevertheless, Elijah was obedient and traveled eighty miles to Sidon. Finding a widow gathering sticks near the gate at Zarephath, he asked her for bread and water. Pessimistically, she said she only has enough food for one meal. *Oops*, Elijah thought, *maybe this is not the widow God had in mind.*

But the widow sacrificially gave what she had to the Jewish prophet. She didn't die of starvation, but rather "she and her household ate for many days" (1 Kings 17:15) from a bowl of flour that was never exhausted. This miracle created a big stir about the God of Israel in Sidon!

What happened here? At Cherith Brook, Elijah had food and water and was safe from Jezebel. He was comfortable. But God's plan required taking a risk — Elijah was to go to Zarephath in Sidon and ask a widow who was about to die for support.

In a similar way, mission workers tell me that fundraising forces them out of comfort and into discomfort. But it is there that they find expanded ministry and expanded funding. And they find an extra measure of God's grace, a supernatural enablement to do what must be done.

Where did Elijah make the most impact? By Cherith Brook alone with the ravens or among strangers at Sidon? As I consider my years of ministry, I say assuredly that God uses me most when I leave my comfort zone and take a risk to interact with new people — even people with whom I feel uncomfortable.

How about you? Where is your Sidon? When do you feel out of your comfort zone? Fundraising? Evangelism? Parenting? During conflict? Public speaking?

2 Corinthians 12:9 says, "My grace is sufficient for you, for power is perfected in weakness." Arise, go to Sidon!

PRAYER

Father of all Comfort, I prefer the friendly confines of my own comfort zones. But as I obey you, I know I need to take risks and confront my discomfort. Still, I hesitate. May I receive your grace daily to launch out like Elijah in ministry and in fundraising. Amen.

5

THE GREATEST OBSTACLE TO FUNDRAISING

When I am afraid, I will put my trust in You. In God whose word I praise, in God I have put my trust; I shall not be afraid. What can mere man do to me?

PSALM 56:3–4

What do mission workers around the world say is the biggest obstacle to raising support?

* Lack of contacts?
* Lack of time?
* Poor economy?

None of these, actually. Mission workers say the biggest obstacle is fear — fear of rejection, fear of failure, and fear of destroying friendships.

Here's the paradox. Missionaries are called by God to do bold spiritual ministry. People look to us for strength. Dare we admit we are fearful?

I discovered today's passage during our first ministry assignment in Iowa City. I was sitting at the kitchen table doing a Bible study on "Fear." From out of nowhere a thought hit me, *Scott, you are a fearful person.* Me? No way. I am a courageous ambassador for Christ in a pagan world!

But the thought persisted.

Then I saw the first word of today's passage: "When." *When* I am afraid, not *if* I am afraid. Even David, the godly Psalmist, admitted he had fears. Slowly, I admitted my fears. I wrote them down one by one, including the names of certain scary people.

Having admitted his fear, David said, "I will put my trust in You." But "Trust in God" is a cliché. Does it mean that God will not allow bad things to happen? Almost humorously, David adds, "What can mere man do to me?"

At your funding appointment, will your prospective giving partner throw his latté at you? No, but even if he does, God is still with you! Our trust is in a sovereign God, no matter how we are treated.

One symptom of inner fear is listening to destructive lies. We whisper to ourselves:

* "Who would want to support me? No one!"
* "She's a single mom, she can't afford to give."
* "People don't actually *like* me."

Before I joined the ministry, I worked for a newspaper selling advertising. One of my clients was Ralph's Grocery, and Ralph had become a friend. But one Monday morning as I got out of my car in Ralph's parking lot, I wondered, *Does Ralph want to see me today? He's busy. I'm probably an annoyance. I'll bet he doesn't even like me.*

So, I got back into the car and drove to my next client at

the camera store. The voice came back, *The camera store guy is too busy to see you. And he doesn't like you either.*

All morning, I listened to the lies. And they paralyzed me. My response? I need chocolate ice cream!

2 Timothy 1:7 says, "For God has not given us a spirit of timidity, but of power and love and of discipline."

Timidity? That's not so bad. Everyone is timid at times. But timidity in Greek (*deilia*), means cowardice. God has not given us a spirit of *cowardice*.

When you received Jesus Christ, you received His Spirit — a Spirit of power, love, and discipline. You did not receive a spirit of cowardice! Instead, boldly write down your fears, and you will be on the way to overcoming them.

When fear strikes you, personalize 2 Timothy 1:7: "God has not given _____ [your name] a spirit of fear. God has given _____ [your name] His Spirit of power, love and discipline!"

It is not wrong to have fear, but it is wrong to live in fear.

PRAYER

Father of truth, I find it difficult to admit that I have fears. But like King David, I now freely admit that I am afraid of _____ and _____. Help me to trust in You and take courage each time I am afraid. Amen.

6

DOES FUNDRAISING WEIGH YOU DOWN?

Tell the sons of Israel to raise a contribution for Me; from every man whose heart moves him you shall raise My contribution.

EXODUS 25:2
(God speaking to Moses on Mount Sinai)

To reduce the angst of fundraising, follow Moses' example. Do you know the story?

Ninety days after leaving Egypt, the Israelites arrived at Mount Sinai, 160 miles southeast. Jutting out of the desert floor, Sinai was enveloped by thick clouds with thunder, lightning, and volcanic smoke. Here, God told Moses *to raise a contribution for Me* to construct a sanctuary that "I may dwell among them" (Exodus 25:8).

Sadly, this was not the first offering project in the desert. When Moses was on Sinai meeting with God, the children of Israel were contributing at the Golden Calf Fundraiser! Aaron told them to "tear off [their] gold rings" to create a golden calf idol (Exodus 32:2). Oops!

Now it was Moses' turn! Did he feel weighed down about asking his fellow desert nomads to give… again? Was fundraising in his job description?

The Sinai example is needed today because many pastors and ministry leaders tip-toe around fundraising in silence and shame. "I don't feel comfortable asking," they say.

What's more, for centuries, fundraising has been sneered at. In the early 1900's John R. Mott traveled tirelessly by train from city to city raising money for the YMCA. He endured much criticism, and said famously, "Blessed are the money-raisers. For in Heaven, they shall sit at the right hand of the martyrs."

No doubt, you feel that pressure. But I wonder, did Moses feel weighed down by asking? Did he *feel* like a martyr? Here are three guidelines to reduce your funding pressure:

1   The Sanctuary Project did not originate with Moses. It was God's idea. And your call to ministry was God's idea too — it did not originate with you.
    Relax!

2   God could have bypassed Moses. Like the Ten Commandments, He could have written His request for gifts on stone tablets. Instead, He instructed Moses to ask for gold, silver, fine linen, porpoise skins, and ten additional items to construct the Tabernacle.

Moses was an intermediary, a catalyst. You too are an intermediary. Like Moses, your job is to share the designs of God with the people of God and invite them to give for the glory of God.

Relax!

3 God could have bypassed the donors just like he could have created a tabernacle by speaking it into existence. But rather, God wanted every man and woman whose heart moved them to share in His work.

Like Moses, you are inviting God's people to participate in God's grand designs. Don't deny them the opportunity!

Relax!

If fundraising continuously weighs you down, something is wrong. Perhaps you forget that you are not the primary player in the threefold process of funding. Biblical fundraising begins and ends with God — as shown here:

* God — He has big ideas that need funding.
* You — Meet with God. Find out what's on His mind. Then boldly invite people to join in *God's work* through giving.
* Givers — They respond as God moves their hearts. No coercion necessary!

You can't do God's calling alone, no more than Moses could build God's tabernacle alone. Moses needed partners. You need partners. And these partners need to be asked. Like Moses, God will give you those whose "hearts move them." You are merely the invitation-giver.

Relax! It's not about you.

PRAYER

God of Mount Sinai, fundraising weighs me down — I'm not sure why.

Perhaps I worry about harming my relationships or hearing "no." I confess that I am probably making it too much about me. Please give me courage to be a bold intermediary in your great Kingdom. Amen.

Day 6

Exodus 25:2

FOOD AND FUNDRAISING

This man receives sinners and eats with them.

LUKE 15:2

This criticism of Jesus was made by the self-righteous Pharisees, the serious Bible teachers of Jesus' day. But their criticism highlights Jesus' love for the lost. How about putting this epitaph on your tombstone! "Here lies [your name]… Dined with Sinners!"

Jesus used dining together as an opportunity to touch the hearts of skeptics. Not counting the two feedings of the multitudes, the Gospels record Jesus sharing meals with others twelve times.

* John 2:1–11   *Wedding feast at Cana*
* Luke 5:27–32   *At Levi's house with his tax collector friends*

Meal gatherings continued in the early church. Acts 2:46 says:

Day by day continuing with one mind in the temple, and breaking bread from house to house, they were taking their meals together with gladness and sincerity of heart.

Food is not only for satisfying hunger. Dining with others lowers defenses, softens hearts, and reduces anxiety. Over meals, memories are made, invitations are given, and hearts are shared.

Often, we don't know what we think about a topic until we talk with someone. Mealtime discussions allow us to know and to be known — to be human with other humans.

But in the West, sales of dinner plates are decreasing and in-home dining areas are becoming obsolete or converted into home offices. At mealtime we hurriedly snarf down snack food at the kitchen counter while fiddling with our phone. Alone. Or we eat fast food in our car... alone.

Let's change that! Dining with potential giving partners

or non-believers in a relaxed atmosphere opens doors and hearts. But here's an embarrassing secret: Mission workers hesitate to invite friends for food because of the cost, or they secretly hope the potential donor will pay.

FOOD AND FUNDRAISING TIPS:

1 If you invite a guest to a restaurant, you buy! It doesn't have to be fancy.
2 Turn off your cell phone for a couple hours. You won't die.
3 Dining in your home lessens cost and deepens bonding with potential donors.
4 Don't hurry to launch your presentation. Become better acquainted. Enjoy the meal. Share your spiritual journey. Ask them to share theirs.
5 Focus the conversation on your potential giving partners. Make it at least 60% about them.

Table manners matter. Pretend your mom is there!

How did Jesus spend His last evening? At a meal with His followers. How will we spend eternity? At the marriage supper of the Lamb (Revelation 19:9).

Jesus wants to dine with you. In Revelation 3:20, He knocks at the door and promises, "I will come in to him and will dine with him, and he with me."

Question: Do two or three potential giving partners come to mind with whom you could share meals? Also, does a non-believer come to mind? You know what to do!

PRAYER

Father, I see that Jesus spent time dining with both friends and skeptics. Help me to be bold enough to invite potential giving partners and non-believers to dine with me, even when I am apprehensive. May the phrase, "dined with sinners," be said of me, too. Amen.

8

EXPECTING OTHERS TO
DO WHAT YOU DO NOT?

You, therefore, who teach another, do you not teach your-self? For the name of God is blasphemed among the Gentiles because of you...

ROMANS 2:21a, 24

As mission workers we are delighted when our partners give monthly — 12 times per year — yes! Extra gifts — yes! Sacrificially — yes! But how about us? Do we give 12 of 12? Do *we* give extra gifts? Do *we* give sacrificially?

As missionaries, we can be lulled into thinking that we are either automatically generous or that biblical generosity applies primarily to non-missionaries.

Early in our marriage, my wife and I pledged month-ly support to a missionary — our first! Sending a gift each month made me proud, my world vision broadened. We were faithful givers…or so we thought.

When we filed our taxes the following January, I found only seven receipts from our mission worker's organization — not twelve. Must be a mistake, I thought, so I double-checked. Nope. Sadly, I only *imagined* we gave every month. This was an embarrassing lesson we determined not to repeat when, later, we became missionaries.

In today's text, Paul accuses the Jewish religious teachers of having a double standard. Do they not *teach themselves*? Furthermore, their misconduct is not merely a private matter, it spills over into public view. The name of God is blasphemed.

Similarly, Jesus said of these teachers:

They say things and do not do them. They tie up heavy burdens and lay them on men's shoulders, but they themselves are unwilling to move them with so much as a finger.
MATTHEW 23:3B, 4

If anyone should practice sacrificial generosity, shouldn't it be those of us in gospel ministry? But some missionaries are not generous. They say, "I give my time." But does giving time excuse us from giving money?

Suppose a wealthy business owner said he cannot join a discipleship Bible study or go to church because he is too busy, but he will make up for it with generous giving. Is that okay?

You know the three T's? Time, Treasure, and Talent. All three should be surrendered to God, of course. No matter which is most natural for us to give, we are still specifically called to give all three. As Christ followers, we shouldn't swap one for another.

In giving financially, the amount is not the issue. You might have less money than a business owner, but give generously of that which God has placed in your hand.

Want to find out if you are generous? Look at your metrics. They are the truth serum of biblical stewardship. Instead of guesstimating, take a moment to accurately calculate what you gave to the Lord's work last year. Include both formal and informal giving. Then calculate that as a percentage of your income. Compare it with previous years. If your income is rising, is your giving also rising?

Expecting others to give generously while you give miserly is hypocrisy. Sooner or later, your secret will go public and harm the gospel.

Former First Lady of the United States Eleanor Roosevelt said famously, "It is not fair to ask of others what you are not willing to do yourself."

How's your giving?

* Do you keep your promises — 12 of 12 months?
* Do you give extra gifts?
* Do you know how much you give? Is it sacrificial?

PRAYER

Lord Jesus Christ, am I guilty of expecting others to do what I am unwilling to do? Perhaps I am unaware. Help me to model consistent, sacrificial generosity — 12 out of 12! May my generosity be a model, not an embarrassment to the gospel. Amen.

9

GIVE AND IT WILL BE GIVEN TO YOU — REALLY?

Give and it will be given to you. They will pour into your lap a good measure — pressed down, shaken together, and running over. For by your standard of measure it will be measured to you in return.

LUKE 6:38

Some preachers have hijacked this verse and made it a formula guaranteeing whopping financial returns for a "seed gift" to their ministry. If you need money — give money. So they say…

Understandably, we are skeptical of Jesus' "promise" about giving — it seems materialistic, a guaranteed financial benefit merely for giving a few dollars? Let's study the context. Look at the powerful verbs starting in verse 28.

* 6:28 *Bless* those who curse you, *pray* for those who mistreat you.
* 6:30 *Give* to everyone who asks of you.
* 6:31 *Treat* others the same way you want them to treat you.
* 6:35 *Love* your enemies, and *do good and lend*, expecting nothing in return.
* 6:36 *Be merciful.*
* 6:37 *Do not judge… do not condemn… pardon, and you will be pardoned.*
* And finally verse 38, *Give.*

Luke 6:28–37 is not primarily about money, but about building Kingdom relationships — especially with those who mistreat you. When we love — even unkind people — when we are merciful and uncondemning, when we seek the other person's good, these same people *pour into our lap* even more love, mercy, and non-condemnation than we originally gave. This is the way of discipleship with Jesus as our leader.

Pour into your lap? The Jews wore a full-length robe that could be pulled up at the waist to form a deep pocket for carrying grain or groceries. Quite a lot could be carried home from the market this way.

What about getting money back? Sure, if money is given, money could come back. But notice verse 35: "expecting nothing in return." *Give and it will be given to you* is not a guaranteed formula to manipulate God into blessing you financially. Jesus' true followers give their whole selves to others without expecting a return.

A missionary was supported with $50 per month for years by "Joe and Cathy" in Arizona, but when Joe lost his job, the support stopped. After a few months, the missionary visited Joe and Cathy, spending two nights in their home and treating them to dinners — the missionary paid! They enjoyed two days of mutual encouragement, laughing, reminiscing, prayer, and Bible study.

When the missionary returned home, the Lord prompted him to send Joe and Cathy $200 — no reason — just because it was needed. Joe wrote back immediately expressing how deeply the $200 gift had encouraged him.

A year passed. Finally, Joe found a good job. Soon the couple re-started support for the missionary, their friend, not for $50 per month, but for $200 per month! What happened here? The missionary genuinely gave of his heart to encourage his *friends*, not to "get something back." But the promise proved true. The $200 per month continues to this day.

My missionary friend, are you giving your whole self to your partners? What are they getting from you besides occasional Mailchimp newsletters?

The people on your mailing list, yes, keep sending them excellent newsletters. But also give them your heart, your emotions, your time, and your money — whatever is needed. And do it one by one! You will find that Jesus' promise holds true. Whatever you give will be *poured into your lap!* Give your whole self, but do it *without expecting anything in return.*

How can you *give* of *yourself* today? With which ministry partner will you begin?

PRAYER

Father in Heaven, sometimes I take my giving partners for granted. Help me to give my emotions, my time, and my energy with the precious friends you have given me. I pray that our investment in each other will glorify your name and advance the Kingdom. Amen.

10

DO YOU HIJACK CONVERSATIONS?

But everyone must be quick to hear, **slow to speak** *and slow to anger.*

JAMES 1:19

Conversation hijacking occurs every day in every culture — especially during funding appointments. To understand hijacking, let's learn from the curious world of bird watching.

As a lifelong birder, I attended a birding convention in Canada with excited fellow bird watchers from North America. After dinner, each person at our table described recent bird sightings from back home — a Great Gray Owl in a Manitoba muskeg marsh, a Lesser Black-backed Gull off the coast of New Hampshire... you get the idea. Exciting birds and wonderful stories!

But one fellow birder ruined every conversation — and he didn't even realize it. Listen in...

Birder A: *We found two Great Gray Owls sitting side-by-side on a frosty morning last week. They were 12 feet up a stunted conifer. No one made a sound. We quietly edged closer to get photos, but then...*

Hijacker: *That's great! My first Great Gray was on a telephone pole right next to the road. He just sat there until a crowd gathered. Then we... [story continues.]*

Birder B: *So, tell us, Birder A, did you get close enough for photos of the Great Gray that cold morning?*

Birder A: *As I was saying, we crept closer and the owl looked at us, but didn't move. Right at that moment, a dog started barking in the distance, and the owl snapped its head in that direction...*

Hijacker: *Once I was photographing a Bald Eagle on a roadside, but a guy driving by honked, and the eagle jumped off its perch. I cussed at the horn honker, but then the eagle circled back to a tree even closer — amazing huh?*

Birder A: *Hmmm...*

What happened here? Let's examine the anatomy of hijacked conversations. The hijacker heard words that jogged his memory of a similar experience, and he couldn't resist sharing that experience when Birder A paused to take a breath. The hijacker was "quick to speak."

We gospel workers are vulnerable to hijacking during fundraising because we are keyed up for the appointment... and we are nervous. We have tons of interesting stuff to say and are looking for any opportunity to begin sharing it. We try to listen, but when our potential donor says something that stirs our memory, we dive in!

Like most conversation hijackers, we don't even realize what we have done. Plus, the more experience we have, the more tempted we are to "contribute." I have done it, and likely so have you.

A friend in Michigan told of a veteran missionary who asked about her family. She was honored he wanted to know. But every few sentences, the missionary jumped in with stories about his own family. Soon, she gave up.

Even godly people hijack conversations. But why do we do it? Let's look a little closer at some of the reasons:

* Insecurity/Self-esteem: Sharing my experience validates my identity. It makes me feel significant.
* Poor People Skills: Some conversationalists don't realize they misread the situation.
* Over-Zealous: Well-intentioned hijackers assume they move the conversation along by introducing their experiences or making points of connection. However, many times, the hijacker puts his own feelings ahead of his listener.

Our text today is the antidote for hijacking: "Be quick to hear, slow to speak…" Before you open your mouth, pause… and pause again. Breathe a two-second prayer. Then ask the Lord if you should speak.

Say to yourself, "Wait! The speaker is going somewhere." Honor her by listening a little bit longer. Don't interrupt what God might be doing. Instead of jumping in with your experience, ask a question to draw out more of her story. Say three little words that honor your conversation partner: "Tell me more!"

PRAYER

Father in Heaven, you are an excellent listener. Thank you for hearing

my Prayers. Please help me to pause...and pause again, and in so do-
ing, to honor others. May I not seek to bolster my ego. Help me not to
hijack conversations. May I be quick to hear and slow to speak. Amen.

Day 10

James 1:19

11

IS THE HOLY SPIRIT INVOLVED IN YOUR FUNDRAISING?

When the Helper comes, whom I will send to you from the Father, that is the spirit of truth who proceeds from the Father, He will testify about Me, and you will testify also, because you have been with Me from the beginning.

JOHN 15:26–27

At a conference of young energetic mission workers, the speaker humorously asked, "If the Holy Spirit went on vacation, how long would you continue doing ministry before you noticed He was gone?"

A nervous chuckle traveled around the audience. But the question stuck with me: Was I aware, hour-by-hour, of the

Holy Spirit's presence in my ministry? Or did I only think of Him when I needed to be bailed out?

Our text today contains a promise about the Holy Spirit that is crucial in the ministry of fundraising.

But first, notice that Jesus refers to the Holy Spirit as *He*, not *it*. "He will testify about Me." The Holy Spirit is not an impersonal force. He is a living being as are other members of the Trinity.

Jesus also called the Holy Spirit, *the helper*. It means *parakletos* in Greek, which is one called alongside to help.[1] Other translations say Comforter (KJV), Counselor (NIV), and Friend (The Message).

Here's the promise: You have a *helper*—*a friend*—who works with you. As *you testify* about Jesus, He also *testifies* about Jesus, going ahead of you, around you, and behind you, whispering to your potential giving partners.

Is the Holy Spirit active in fundraising? Yes! And yes again! I've heard story after story of "coincidences" that can only be attributed to the Spirit's work. For example, many missionaries have told me that when they phone potential giving partners to ask for a meeting, the response is, "It's interesting you called today—we were just talking about you yesterday."

Another example is a new ministry worker who came for fundraising training in Colorado Springs; he was fearful. Before the first meeting, he went to the Broadmoor Hotel and sat by the lake finishing his Bible study assignment, praying, and journaling. His funding goal was in the "impossible" category: $26,000. Then he got the wild idea to write a letter sharing his apprehensions about fundraising. He folded the draft of the letter and placed it on a bench with a stone on top so it wouldn't blow away. Then he left for his first training meeting ten miles across town.

Later that day, a married couple vacationing from Texas found the note, drove to the training location, and gave this surprised mission worker a $1,000 check for his new ministry!

At another funding seminar, a young couple with a baby had set an appointment with a longtime friend. Arriving at their friend's house, they took a few minutes to get the baby and the baby carrier out of the car. Meanwhile, the homeowner was watching from his window and came out to ask if everything was okay. But he was a stranger — they had gone to the wrong address! They apologized and started to leave.

But discovering they were missionaries, the stranger invited them into his house, listened to their ministry dreams, and became a giving partner!

Friend, during your busy days of fundraising, are you aware of your wonderful *helper*? Who should be on your Top 25 Prospects list? Ask the Holy Spirit. When you run out of contacts, where do you go next? Ask Him. He goes before you on every phone call, and He sits with you at every meeting. Count on it!

PRAYER

Father in Heaven, I confess that I often forget about the Holy Spirit's presence as my wonderful counselor. Help me to be aware of what He is doing in my fundraising. I welcome His testifying about Jesus as I testify about Jesus. Thank you for this gracious gift. Amen.

12

HOW WAS JESUS FUNDED?

The twelve were with Him, and also some women who had been healed of evil spirits and sicknesses: Mary who was called Magdalene...and Joanna the wife of Chuza, Herod's steward, and Susanna, and many others who were contributing to their support out of their private means.

LUKE 8:1b-3

How did Jesus fund His ministry?

* Lived on the streets as a beggar?
* Worked as a carpenter?
* Miraculously multiplied loaves and fishes daily?
* We don't know...?

Actually, we *do* know. Our text today shows that Jesus was funded by women who had been touched by His ministry —

Mary Magdalene, Joanna, Susanna, and *many others who were contributing to their support...*

This takes the mystery out of how Jesus lived day to day. Of the 2,000–3,000 meals Jesus ate during His three-year ministry, only three times is it recorded that He miraculously provided food — the feeding of the 4,000, the feeding of the 5,000, and turning water into wine at Cana.

Even though Luke 9:58 says, "The Son of Man has nowhere to lay His head," there is no evidence that He lived on the street. Jesus was an itinerant preacher — not an itinerant beggar.

If ever anyone did *not* need financial support, it was Jesus! Could not the one who created the world, owns the cattle on a thousand hills (Psalm 50:10), and provided bread and fish for 5,000 have funded Himself? Instead, the Son of God held back His miraculous powers and lived with humble dependence on His giving partners. That's how the Godhead planned it from the beginning. Jesus' funding model did not happen by accident!

Let's also pause to take notice that Jesus' funding model is not merely about cash flow. God wants *people* involved in His worldwide Kingdom work! If Jesus had funded Himself, Magdalene, Joanna, Susanna, and *many others* would have been denied the honor of participating in God's work.

For 2,000 years, millions of believers have been blessed as they partnered financially with gospel workers from Jerusalem to Irian Jaya to Uzbekistan.

Once, a school teacher was called to serve Christ as a two-year missionary to Russia. To avoid the scary prospect of fundraising, she decided to fund herself by taking money from her savings account — the entire two-year amount. But her own mother called her out: "Don't you dare support yourself. Being your financial partner is the only way *I* will ever get to Russia!"

What does Jesus' funding model imply for us today? Humility, for one thing. Our human nature disdains relying on others. Growing up on a farm, I was proud that our family (like many others) never asked for help. But Jesus lived in dependence on others—not as a beggar, but as a Kingdom worker with like-minded partners. If the Son of God lived a life of dependence, so must we.

Jesus' funding model is reproducible; it *will* work for you! Ask God to give you many partners, starting with those whose lives you have touched, even though it may be few. Give them the privilege of joining the ranks of Magdalene, Joanna, Susanna, and many others.

PRAYER

Father, sometimes fundraising feels like begging—not sure why I feel that way. But I see that Jesus, the King of the Universe, was not a beggar and was humbly dependent on others as partners. Please enable me to live joyfully dependent on you through the partners you bring my way. Give me grace to start with those whose lives I have touched—even in small ways. I count on you to multiply it from there. Amen.

13

FUNDRAISING AND SELF-CRITICISM

We will know by this that we are of the truth, and will assure our heart before Him in whatever our heart condemns us; for God is greater than our heart and knows all things.

1 JOHN 3:19–20

As a gospel worker, you are conscientious. You are sensitive to spiritual promptings — that's good! But what happens if you become *overly* conscientious and find yourself wallowing in self-criticism?

Today's culture tells you to "follow your heart." But is that always wise? Our text reminds us that this heart of ours *condemns us* and attacks us. For example, our heart whispers, *You think that you can reach 100 percent of budget? Hah —*

no way! You're don't have what it takes! And parenting? Hah!
And what about your lethargic prayer life? Hah!

Negative self-talk is destructive! Your heart is an unfair accuser with whom you can never win an argument. No matter how sincere your intentions, your heart will find fault with you, even as you pray. Late author Brennan Manning (1934–2013) wrote in *Abba's Child,* "In my experience, self-hatred is the dominant malaise crippling Christians and stifling their growth in the Holy Spirit." [2]

Every day, like an underground sewage pipe, your heart (or conscience) floods your mind with condemnations. Do you recognize these subtle attacks? Do you think they come from God?

Our text reminds us that *God is greater than our heart.* Our heart is not the final authority. Let us not confuse condemnation by our heart with conviction by the Holy Spirit. John 16:8 says:

And He [the Holy Spirit], when He comes, will convict the world concerning sin and righteousness and judgment...

The Holy Spirit *convicts* us of sin. He doesn't *condemn* us for being sinners, as this diagram shows.

	Heart	Holy Spirit
Self-talk message	Condemnation	Conviction
Target	Attacks your personhood	Points out a specific sin
Remedy	None — no hope	Confess — make things right

Do you see the difference? The heart's condemnation attacks your identity — you are a bad fundraiser or a bad parent, a total failure! But the Holy Spirit identifies a specific sin and helps make things right.

For example, perhaps at your funding appointment yesterday, you exaggerated the number of people in Bible studies in order to impress the donor. Afterward, you couldn't get that out of your mind, and wish you could take it back. When the Holy Spirit convicts, we know what to confess. And we feel clean.

But with condemnation we can do nothing to change. We just feel rotten.

Furthermore, does your heart tell the truth? Are those condemning thoughts accurate? No, says Jeremiah 17:9: "The heart is more deceitful than all else and desperately sick; who can understand it?" Beware that your heart can mislead you.

Our heart doesn't know all things. But God *does* know all things. Therefore, we resort to Him for final analysis. Our conscience is not God, nor should our conscience ever be considered greater than God.

If you pay attention to your heart's self-condemning thoughts, you will constantly feel guilty, tired, and discouraged. You will be tempted to give up not only in fundraising, but in everything. Don't give false guilt the upper hand!

When a self-critical thought pops into your mind, analyze it prayerfully. Is it a self-loathing criticism attacking your personhood? Or a nudge from the Holy Spirit about a specific sin? The Holy Spirit doesn't condemn your entire being. *God is greater than your heart*, so listen to Him.

There is now no condemnation for those who are in Christ Jesus.

ROMANS 8:1

PRAYER

Father of liberty, I admit that I pay too much attention to the accusa-

tions of my heart. Please help me to distinguish between my condemn-
ing self-thoughts and conviction by the Holy Spirit. Help me listen for
the Spirit's prompting and tune out the noise of self-loathing. Amen.

Day 13

1 John 3:19–20

14

YOUR BIBLE OR
YOUR OPINIONS?

For the word of God is living and active and sharper than
any two-edged sword, and piercing as far as the division of
soul and spirit, of both joints and marrow, and able to judge
the thoughts and intentions of the heart.

HEBREWS 4:12

The Francis Schaeffer Institute of Church Leadership Development determined that 72 percent of pastors study the Bible *only* for preparing sermons or lessons. A similar study revealed that "90 percent of pastors say they are frequently fatigued and worn out..."[3]

We understand! Gospel workers must deliver God's manna to others. But do we allow time for the Bible to speak to us personally, to touch our sacred opinions...especially our opinions about fundraising?

If you google "fundraising," you will find tons of advice, much of it helpful. But does it speak to the *intentions of your heart* or your opinions regarding money?

I would not be in ministry today were it not for the Bible. My personal opinions were strong, but they were wrong. Here's what happened:

In our early days of university ministry, students were coming to Christ. Sensing God's call on my life, I quit my job at the newspaper and launched into "full-time" ministry. My skeptical newspaper boss quizzed me, "How will you finance yourself?"

I beamed, "Not to worry! The Lord will provide."

But the Lord *did not* provide! A few friends sent monthly support, and a few others sent sympathy gifts. We lived frugally, but with two little kids, we couldn't pay our bills. My common-sense fundraising opinions included:

* Focus on ministry, money will follow automatically.
* Send letters asking people to pray, don't ask them to give.
* Cut, cut, cut spending.

Behind on our bills and feeling desperate, I turned to "hinting" about finances in nearly all my daily conversations. I felt like a beggar.

Finally, I turned to the Bible. I looked up "fundraising" in the concordance — nothing. But day by day, hoping beyond hope, I ransacked the Bible. One day I discovered Numbers 18:21–24, the next day Luke 8:1–3. Soon fundraising passages tumbled toward me. Wow!

God humbled me. His Word *judged the thoughts and intentions of my heart.* I let go of my arrogant opinions and put the Scriptures into action. Our donor income began to rise.

Living and active indeed!

Our passage today says the Bible is *able to judge the*

thoughts and intentions of our heart. Your supervisor, your friends, even your family might not know your true motives — especially in money matters — but God knows. We have no place to hide.

In each country where I teach Biblical Fundraising (BFR), I ask: "What is your biggest benefit from this training?" The answers are always the same: "The personal Bible study assignments" and "Studying the fundraising verses *for myself.*"

Australian theologian J. Sidlow Baxter (1903–1999) used to say that every Christian worker ought to be a Bible specialist.

How about you? Is the Bible *living and active* in your life today? Are you becoming a specialist in the Bible?

Questions for application:

* How about slowing down to enjoy the Bible, not for others, but *just for you?*
* When in your daily schedule can you take time to be alone with the Bible's Author?
* Are there any financial opinions you need to change or drop?

PRAYER

Father in Heaven, I confess that I often pay more attention to my own common sense or to fundraising advice than to the Bible. Help me to come to your Word just as I am, not to prepare for others, but to enjoy your presence myself. May your Word be living and active in me. Amen.

15

RELATIONSHIP PROBLEMS AND FUNDRAISING

I urge Euodia and I urge Syntyche to live in harmony in the Lord. Indeed, true companion, I ask you also to help these women who have shared my struggle in the cause of the gospel...

PHILIPPIANS 4:2–3a

Two members of the Philippian fellowship were quarreling — Euodia and Syntyche. And they were not immature new Christians — they were mature fellow-workers who had *shared [Paul's] struggle in the cause of the gospel.* Were they in disharmony about a ministry issue, an unkind word? Whatever their quarrel, large or small, Paul heard about it 500 miles away in Rome.

Sadly, quarreling in ministry continues today. The most

common problem in missions is not learning a language or adjusting to a culture. Rather it is missionaries *quarreling* among themselves. And this before a watching world!

What does this have to do with fundraising? Plenty! When disputing with a colleague, your mind can think of nothing else! Your emotions are in a frenzy with constant mental arguing, as you replay it over and over.

So…set a funding appointment? Thank a donor? Write a newsletter? Our distraught minds reply, "Not today!"

Let's follow Paul's advice for handling quarrels.

1 *Confront the issue.* Paul didn't sweep this dispute under the rug. Don't merely swallow hard and keep going. Ignoring disharmony is bad practice and not acceptable from a biblical perspective.

Sadly, many gospel workers today grew up in homes where relational difficulties were ignored, similar to one-celled amoebas edging their way around an obstacle rather than confronting it.

About this passage, Bible commentator William Barclay said, "A quarreling church is no church at all, for it is one from which Christ has been shut out." [4]

2 *Talk in private.* Paul urges Euodia and Syntyche to sort it out, just between the two of them. Let us talk *to* one another, not *about* one another.

Jesus said, "If your brother sins, go and show him his sin in private" (Matthew 18:15). Note: "Show him his sin" does not mean cuss him out. Simply explain exactly what he or she did or said that affected you. Don't judge motives or give a sermonette.

I like to start with the question: "May I tell you how I feel about….?"

3 *Bring in a third-party peace maker if needed.* Paul calls on an unnamed *true companion* (perhaps Epa-

phroditus who carried this letter) to help Euodia and Syntyche.

4   *Seek to live in harmony in the Lord.* What does the harmony mentioned in Philippians chapter 4 look like? Agreeing on everything? *Living in harmony*, like singing in harmony, means each voice contributes its unique part. Our voices are different, but we sing the same song! Your voice is needed. And your disagreeable colleague's voice is also needed.

Here's a classic story told by mission pioneer, former Navigator International Director Lorne Sanny. During a busy week of meetings, Lorne said he awoke one morning under intense pressure, and without meaning it, he spoke harshly to his wife.

Driving to the office, Lorne rationalized aloud: "I didn't exactly *explode.* I just threw my weight around in my own home." But God's Spirit persisted. Lorne immediately stopped to call Lucy and apologize. It was so important that he didn't even wait until he reached his office!

How about you? Do you need to stop your busy life today and clear the air with a colleague? Does a name come to mind? Don't sweep it under the rug.

PRAYER

Sovereign Lord, I confess that some of my colleagues and leaders annoy me. And I confess I spend precious minutes mentally arguing with them. Please forgive me and help me to focus on their strengths rather than what I don't like about them. Please give me grace and timing to sort it out privately with them. Amen.

16

CAN MISSIONARIES SAVE? HOW?

There is precious treasure and oil in the dwelling of the wise,
but a foolish man swallows it up.

PROVERBS 21:20

Missionaries want to save, and someday they will. Someday. But how can they? Their donor income is often meager, and it bounces up and down. In Africa, urgent financial pleas from family or friends whisk away cash intended for saving. And some ask, "Does a savings account show distrust in God?"

Today's text is blunt! It presents two extremes:

* Wise versus foolish.
* Accumulation versus immediate spending.

The wise have *precious treasure and oil* in their dwellings. Middle class people often poke fun of the "idle rich" and assume that their *treasure and oil* (wealth) comes from inheritance.

But the world is changing. Today in America, only 21 percent of those with a net worth of $1 million inherited any of it.[5] That means 79 percent reached a net worth of $1 million through accumulation, month-by-month, year-by-year. The popular belief that today's millionaires are those who inherited wealth is untrue.

Precious treasure and oil come not primarily through inheritance but through gradual accumulation. By contrast, foolish people *swallow it up* — which indicates immediate consumption. When it comes to spending, the wise have a small vocabulary: "No!"

This teaching is 3,000 years old! It assumes saving is wise. Don't swallow up *all* you earn.

My friend Nelson from Zambia said that each year his village set aside a portion of the corn crop as seed for the following year. To prevent thievery, the seed-corn cobs were stored in a secure hut with a tiny opening — only a small boy could enter. Even if the village was hungry, the seed was not touched.

As a toddler, Nelson was chosen by the villagers to be boosted into the hut opening to pass out the seed at planting time. As his bare feet melted into the cool corn, he experienced firsthand the importance of saving. He never forgot it.

But Jesus said, "Do *not* store up for yourselves treasures on earth..." So, what is the difference between saving and hoarding?

We have a clue from Joseph in Egypt. He was warned that seven good years would be followed by seven years of famine. During the good years Joseph stored grain in abundance, like "the sand of the sea."

Then came famine. Genesis 41:57 says, "The people of all

the earth came to Egypt to buy grain from Joseph, because the famine was severe…"

Joseph had a godly purpose for saving — the coming famine. That's the difference between biblical saving and hoarding. To avoid hoarding, ask:

What are my *godly purposes* for saving?

* Preparing for emergency?
* Purchasing a reliable vehicle?
* Kid's schooling?
* Aging parents?
* Future seed to grow crops?

In our early years of marriage with a growing family, my wife and I tried to save. We deposited our paycheck on Friday, paid our bills, and bought groceries, but we were broke by noon Monday! We lived frugally, but there was never enough left over to save.

"Someday we will save," we always said.

Then similar to the Zambian villagers, we tried PYF — Pay Yourself First. We deposited our paycheck on Friday and simultaneously transferred a small amount of money to a separate savings account. We now had a little less to spend and I thought we would die. (We didn't!) In setting aside money each week, we felt control over our finances. No more living paycheck to paycheck.

Someday is today! Even if you're not fully funded, determine your godly purposes, then set aside a small amount each payday. See what happens. See what *God* will do for *you!*

PRAYER

Owner of the cattle on a thousand hills, please guide me to the godly purposes for which I need precious treasure and oil. May I manage my income with discipline rather than swallowing it up. Amen.

17

ASKING WITHOUT SHAME

Then the king said to me, "What would you request?" So I prayed to the God of Heaven.

NEHEMIAH 2:4

I have yet to meet a mission worker who has not struggled with "asking." That includes me, especially in my early days. Ministry leaders are bold when it comes to believing God for changed lives. But asking others to give? They wilt like sautéed spinach in a sizzling pan.

Buried in our DNA is the idea that if we truly trusted God, we would not need to "lower ourselves to beg" for funding. Plus, it feels like friends and family look down on us. "Get a real job!" they say. Or they quietly wonder if we will embarrass ourselves — or them.

Other advisors tell us stories about miraculous last-minute funds that arrived for their ministry *without* any embarrassing asking. "Don't ask, just pray. Tell only God," they say. "Telling only God" is attractive because it avoids the risk of embarrassment and rejection.

The underlying issue is shame. The Lily Foundation out of Indianapolis says, "A shroud of silence and shame surrounds ministry and money." What is shame? A painful emotion caused by a strong sense of guilt, embarrassment, unworthiness, or disgrace.

A generous business friend in Minneapolis described missionary shame:

These missionaries shuffle timidly into my office hoping for funding. Their heads hang down, they mumble something about their ministry. They are embarrassed to ask me to give for their project. So I bark at them, "Get your head up! Look me in the eye. Stop looking at your shoes and tell me what you need."

He's right!

In our passage today, as chief wine steward to the Persian King Artaxerxes, Nehemiah had much to fear, but he kept his head up. He boldly asked the king for permission to re-

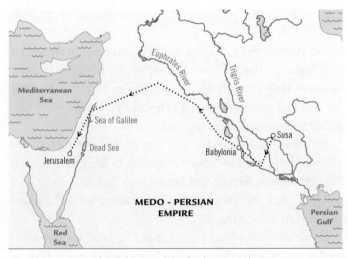

Nehemiah's expedition back to Jerusalem

build the wall of Jerusalem 750 miles away. And he didn't stop there. He also asked for travel documents to proceed safely through Persian lands on the way to Jerusalem. And finally, he asked for timber from the king's forest with which to rebuild.

And he was humble. He said in verse 5, "If it please the king…"

Nehemiah was not ashamed, but he was probably afraid. Our text says he "prayed to the God of Heaven" in the heat of the battle, just before he asked! He did not let fear or shame hold him back.

Here are four additional examples of *asking* to advance God's kingdom. Did these leaders ask with their heads down?

* Moses asked the Israelites to give for the desert tabernacle. (Exodus 35:1–9)
* Elijah asked a Gentile widow for support. (1 Kings 17)
* Paul asked the Roman Christians to fund his ministry to Spain. (Romans 15:20–24)
* Jesus instructed the twelve and the seventy to seek worthy hosts for lodging. (Matthew 10:5–15 and Luke 10:1–12)

These all asked boldly, and so can you — so *must* you! Biblical fundraising is not begging. In Jesus' words, you are "worthy of support" (Matthew 10:10).

Notice that Moses' appeal was not about Moses. Nehemiah's appeal was not about Nehemiah. If you are ashamed to invite others to join you in ministry, is it because there is too much "you" in your appeal?

You are called by God to advance His worldwide Kingdom. Put away feelings of shame. You may be fearful, but like Nehemiah, humbly and boldly ask!

Get your head up! You have the solution to the world's problems!

PRAYER

Creator of all, sometimes I cringe in asking people to give. It feels shameful and sub-spiritual. I wish money would come without my having to ask. But you have given me a special calling. Please help me to ask humbly and boldly. I will pray Nehemiah's short fundraising prayer in the process. I'm depending on you. Amen.

18

GET A REAL JOB!

[Don't take] a bag for your journey, or even two coats or [two pair of] sandals or a staff, for the worker is worthy of his [or her] support.

MATTHEW 10:10

Have you been asked the "real job" question?

A missionary's best friend scolded him saying, "Why don't you get a real job? Get out of this ministry stuff!" An African father told his son-in-law, "It is a waste for you to go into ministry while Africa needs your university training."

Our environment doesn't help. Your church culture might esteem church pastors but disdain missionaries. "Too bad," skeptical friends say, "she could have gone far given her university training."

No wonder many Christian workers feel devalued.

If your family and friends affirm your calling — wonderful! But that won't sustain you. This is an *identity issue*. How you think about yourself is crucial!

In our passage today, Jesus is sending out the twelve disciples to villages around Israel. He tells them *not* to take:

* A bag (Greek *pera*) for carrying provisions, but *pera* also denotes a beggar's collecting bag.
* Two coats or [extra] sandals. An extra coat could double as a nighttime covering. Jesus did not expect his emissaries to spend nights in the open field.
* Staff. It's a symbol of authority. Go without pomp or religious accoutrement.

By saying, "Don't take a beggar's bag nor expect to sleep outdoors," Jesus did not allow his ambassadors to have a beggar's mentality. Then He states a principle: *the worker is worthy of his [or her] support.*" He said it again in Luke chapter 10 when he sent out the seventy.

Twenty years later, the Apostle Paul confronted the Corinthian church's question: Do ministers have a right to receive financial support? Paul answered by paraphrasing Jesus. "So also the Lord directed those who proclaim the gospel to get their living from the gospel" (1 Corinthians 9:14).

Similarly, in 1 Timothy 5:17–18 on the issue of what to pay church leaders, Paul quotes Jesus word for word, "The laborer is worthy of his wages." For 20 years Jesus' followers repeated this financial teaching all the way to Paul's generation — the worker is worthy of support.

This biblical principle still applies today. You are not asking for alms. You are not saying, "Please, sir, times are tough, can you help me out?" By contrast, you are inviting people to partner in the greatest adventure on Earth: advancing the gospel of Christ to your countrymen who have no hope.

A young gospel worker from Zambia scheduled her first funding appointment with her former boss, a genial and respected businessman from her church. With high hopes she shared her ministry vision. But the man's tone quickly changed. He said, "Why don't you get a real job?" In her own words…

I felt numb and discouraged. He then told me that I was brainwashed and needed to wake up to reality. He dismissed the idea of me being a missionary [since] I was not Western. He [said] that I'd let down my family by choosing to throw away my education and accepting poverty [by living as a missionary.]

When he finally finished, I gathered up what little courage I had left and said, "Sir, I do have a real job with a real employer, and my job is sharing the gospel to Zambia."

You, too, have a real job — serving the king of the universe!

PRAYER

Father, you have called me to ministry, but some days I feel devalued. Sometimes in my heart, I feel like a beggar. I choose to believe I am **worthy of support**. *Please help me to live in that identity. Amen.*

19

OVERWHELMED?

Therefore let us draw near with confidence to the throne of grace, so that we may receive mercy and find grace to help in time of need.

HEBREWS 4:16

A young gospel worker's first weeks in fundraising were exciting, but then the "yeses" slowed down. Months passed with little change. Exasperated, he said, "I can't imagine *gutting out* fundraising for the next two months — not to mention the next two years! For a lifetime? No way!"

If this were your friend, how would you encourage him? How about a pep talk like, "God's work done in God's way never lacks God's supply!" Hmmm…

Our passage today speaks to us when we are overwhelmed, not only in fundraising, but anytime we are at our wit's end.

First, we draw near not to the throne of "try harder," but

to the *throne of grace*. What is *grace*? The popular acronym G-R-A-C-E — God's Riches At Christ's Expense — is a wonderful way to describe this theological truth.

But let's take G-R-A-C-E one step further with an expanded definition:

Day 19

Hebrews 4:16

Grace: "Supernatural enablement to do what must be done whether you feel like it or not."

"Supernatural enablement" may be called upon for setting fundraising appointments, leading a Bible study of digitally distracted teens, or when you are obligated to attend a ballet recital of your cousin's three-year-old.

Grace is not merely a theological concept assuring sinners of heaven. Grace is also available when you have zero energy to do what must be done — like making a funding call you've been postponing.

Grace to help is not gutting it out, nor is it trying harder with a better attitude. Grace empowers you to do what must be done far out of proportion to your meager supply of energy. You were fully saved by grace…and you'll be fully funded by grace!

In time of need. God doesn't give grace in advance; it can't be stored up like a capacitor stores electricity. Grace springs forth when you are desperate, often in the nick of time. For example, if you can't imagine doing fundraising for the next umpteen weeks, that's okay. God has not given you grace *today* to deal with the next umpteen weeks. Don't be so hard on yourself!

A colleague felt overwhelmed by a ministry project he had postponed for weeks, and the deadline was coming fast. He needed to assign 1,000 ministry contact-cards in Wisconsin to volunteers. It was mind-numbing work.

Glaring at the boxes of cards sitting on the floor of his study, he finally prayed, "Lord, I don't have it in me to tackle this project, but I will start. I ask for your grace to help. This is my time of need."

Without enthusiasm, he lugged the boxes down to his basement, spread the 1,000 cards on a ping-pong table and began sorting them. Three hours later, he was loving it! Grace supplied in his time of need!

In similar fashion, I once procrastinated for weeks to set fundraising appointments. Plus, I was not feeling close to the Lord. Finally, I prayed, "Lord, I feel too lethargic to talk to potential donors, but I will give it forty-five minutes, then I'm stopping." Two hours later, I had five appointments and didn't want to stop.

You don't have to muster up artificial enthusiasm to do the difficult task before you. God promises to supply *grace to help in time of need*. Now is your time of need! Draw near with confidence!

PRAYER

God of grace, thank you that I don't have to manufacture faith in advance for the next two months or two years — please give me supernatural enablement for the next two minutes. Now is my time of need. May I experience your G-R-A-C-E as I confidently approach your throne of grace. Amen.

20

THE FOUR D'S OF DISCOURAGEMENT

Do not call me Naomi; call me Mara, for the Almighty has dealt very bitterly with me. I went out full, but the Lord has brought me back empty.

RUTH 1:20-21

Discouragement in fundraising doesn't "suddenly happen!" It's a process. And you can recover more quickly if you understand the Four D's.

In our text today, Naomi, the mother-in-law of Ruth (great grandmother of King David), became so discouraged that she changed her name. Naomi means "pleasant" in Hebrew, but Naomi said, *"Call me Mara."* "Mara" has a Jewish history. After escaping Egypt, the Israelites traveled three days into the Sinai wilderness, but found no water. Finally, at an oasis called Marah they found water, but it was bitter and undrinkable — a huge disappointment. Reflecting on that story, "pleasant Naomi" changed her name to Mara — she had become bitter.

Here is Naomi's journey (and ours) through the Four D's of Discouragement:

DISAPPOINTMENT

Discouragement starts with *disappointment*. Indeed, discouragement is not possible without the beginning feelings of disappointment.

And Naomi had three. First, her husband Elimelech died unexpectedly in the land of Moab. Second, her two sons married Moabite girls, not Jews. And third, the sons died (Ruth 1:3–5). Naomi is left with no means of livelihood and two Moabite daughters-in-law.

Your disappointment(s) may not be as devastating as Naomi's, but even small setbacks are hurtful. Consider the

following scenario: your last fundraising appointment went well. You listened, told stories, and didn't panic when you made the appeal. The donor couple cheerfully said they would pray about a monthly gift. You left nearly certain they would say yes to becoming a giving partner, but when you checked back a couple days later, they said no, without explanation. Disappointment.

DOUBT

Disappointment leads to *doubt*. Scripture doesn't describe Naomi's doubts, but she probably wondered, *Why did we move to Moab? Why did my sons marry Moabites? What did I do wrong?*

Similarly, in funding, we ask, "What did I do wrong?" We replay the appointment over and over, doubting and second-guessing the way it transpired.

DISILLUSIONMENT

At this stage, we lose objectivity. We see that in Naomi — she changed her name to Mara which means "bitter."

Besides losing objectivity, we question our motives, "What made me think I could raise 100 percent support? I'll never be up to budget."

We become disillusioned not only with fundraising, but, like Naomi, with life itself. We think, "Not only am I a terrible fundraiser, I'm a terrible Christian! And I thought I could be a missionary? Ha!" We forget the strength of God's calling on our lives.

DISCOURAGEMENT

Now, full-fledged discouragement sets in. Fundraising is bad. Ministry is bad. Even the weather is bad. We mope around feeling useless and wish we had gone into business with a distant uncle in Kansas City.

And we long to escape. King David said, "Oh that I had wings like a dove! I would fly away and be at rest" (Psalm 55:6). Similarly, we fly away to hobbies or social media. Fleshly temptations, such as over-eating, over-sleeping, and sexual sin also become more tempting.

The Four D's help us identify where we are in the discouragement process. But we recover more quickly if we can identify the specific disappointment.

How about you? What exactly was it that crushed you? Hearing a "no" will happen again, I'm sorry to say. But is it the end of the world? Does your disappointment deserve the emotional energy you're giving it?

The Four D's of Discouragement

1 Peter 5:7 says, "Casting all your anxiety upon Him, because He cares for you." Identify the disappointment, grieve over it, give it to the Lord, and move on.

And whatever you do, don't change your name!

Ruth 1:20–21

PRAYER

Father, help me identify the disappointment that caused me to drift down to Discouragement Town. Help me keep my disappointments in perspective. May I not forget who I am in You. By your grace, I will not become bitter. Amen.

21

THE POWER OF PERSONAL ATTENTIVENESS

Though I have many things to write to you, I do not want to do so with paper and ink; but I hope to come to you and speak face to face, so that [our] joy may be made full.
2 JOHN 12

In 1999, Colin Powell, former U.S. Military Chief of Staff, pleaded with an audience in Washington D.C. to help economically deprived young people. He said that it would take more than just buying them computers. His plea was that each young person needed and deserved personal attentiveness.

And giving personal attentiveness succeeded. Powell said:

You should see those kids being tutored by old retired geezers at my church... [They] are saying, "White people are not the enemies...they spend their Saturday mornings with me." [6]

There's a lesson here for fundraisers. One-on-one personal attentiveness gets results that mass mailings, flashy dinners, and social media posts cannot.

In our text today, the Apostle John wanted to *speak face to face* with church leaders in Asia Minor rather than write with *paper and ink.* The *many things* he wanted to talk about surely included "deceivers who have gone out into the world" (2 John, verse 7). These heretics taught that Jesus was simply a spirit, not a physical being. He only "seemed" real. Today, we call it docetism.

John is aware that words on paper can be misconstrued. Serious matters like docetism need face-to-face speaking.

Proverbs 27:17 is similar: "Iron sharpens iron, so one man [or woman] sharpens another." This analogy is of a farm implement — metal rubbing against metal. *Iron* sharpens *iron.* But creampuffs do not sharpen creampuffs!

Do you want to sharpen your donors? Do you want them to sharpen you? One-on-one personal attentiveness is the secret. John added that speaking face-to-face causes *joy to be made full.*

But besides mutual sharpening, face-to-face communication creates emotional bonding.

Have you ever supported a missionary and not received a *personal* acknowledgment of your gift? How did you feel?

A few years ago, we started partnering with a missionary at $100 per month. After our first gift, we assumed we'd receive some sort of personal acknowledgment — a thank-you note, phone call, or text. But...nothing. Did he even receive the gift, we wondered?

Soon after, he did add us to his mailing list. That was a good sign, but his newsletters gave thanks to his large group of donors. We never received a personal word.

Sadly, this is the norm for many mission workers. They

thank the "group." They send news to the "group." But without personal attentiveness, donor bonding decreases and attrition increases.

Giving decisions are emotional decisions. When you give your partners one-by-one personal attention, you engage their emotions. Suddenly they feel important, like they make a difference. Their commitment to you is deepened in ways that group mailings cannot achieve.

What about Jesus? Though He taught thousands and spent hours with the twelve disciples, He took time to seek out and minister to individuals one at a time.

He gave personal attentiveness to the woman at the well and to Nicodemus at night. He walked privately with Peter after the resurrection by the Sea of Galilee.

Plus, after healing a man born blind, the angry Jews kicked the now-seeing man out of the synagogue. John 9:35 says, "Jesus heard that they had put [the blind man] out, and *finding him,* He said, 'Do you believe in the Son of Man?'"

Jesus went and found the man!

Are you tapping into the power of personal attentiveness?

PRAYER

Dear Lord God, I confess I count on my group letters to show appreciation to my donors. Help me take time to connect personally with each one now and then. May I follow the Apostle John's example of speaking face to face. And may full joy be the result — for them and for me. Amen.

22

HOW MUCH SHOULD YOU BE PAID?

The elders who rule well are to be considered worthy of double honor, especially those who work hard at preaching and teaching. For the Scripture says, "You shall not muzzle the ox while he is threshing," and "The laborer is worthy of his wages."

1 TIMOTHY 5:17–18
(Paul speaking to Timothy, a pastor at Ephesus)

Where is it written that missionaries and pastors are supposed to be poor? Must you take a vow of poverty when you enter the Lord's service, as practiced during the Middle Ages? Even today, in most countries, it is assumed that if you go into ministry you will be "poor as a church mouse."

Sadly, many missionaries in the past accepted and perpetuated this idea. They didn't expect to be adequately paid, and many were not. But the next generation of mission workers is questioning that. Let's look to the Scripture for this important topic.

Should ministry workers be poor? Fasten your seatbelt for Paul's instruction to Pastor Timothy.

1 *Double Honor.* The Greek word is *timao*, a financial term meaning "price or value." An honorary plaque and a round of applause at a pie supper does *not* describe *timao.*

Though not precisely defined, *double honor* leans toward generous rather than stingy pay. It could refer to paying double what church widows at Ephesus were paid for their informal, part-time ministry. (1 Timothy 5:3–16).

2 *Rule Well, Work Hard:* A first-grade student was asked what he wanted to be when he grew up. He said, "A preacher. I'd only have to work one hour per week." The church at Ephesus had grown to the point of needing ruling elders and preaching elders. They surely worked more than one hour per week.

Paul doesn't say all elders should receive double honor — only those who *rule well* or *work hard* at preaching and teaching. Not everyone was paid the same, but the implication is clear: those who *work hard* and *rule well* should be paid generously.

Reminder! Being called to ministry does not give you permission to be slothful. Do you *work hard*? Because those who support you work hard!

3 *Scripture Says.* Not presenting his own opinion, Paul quotes Moses and Jesus.

In Deuteronomy 25:4, Moses commanded the Jews not to muzzle their oxen as they walked in circles threshing out grain. This verse is also quoted in our kitchen to justify pre-dinner sampling.

Jesus instructed the disciples in Luke 10:7 and Matthew 10:10, "The laborer is worthy of his wages." Jesus spoke this twenty years before Paul came on the scene. An important teaching passed down year by year to Paul.

Jesus is drawing from Old Testament teaching. For example:

* "You shall give him his wages on his day before the sun sets" (Deuteronomy 24:15). Pay him promptly.
* Jeremiah preached against using "his neighbor's services without pay" (Jeremiah 22:13).

Where is it written that gospel workers should be paid poorly? Not in the Bible! Jesus cares about His work and His workers. You are worthy of support. Today's health-and-wealth preachers use these texts to justify extravagant incomes with flamboyant lifestyles. That is not what we are talking about. We are talking about establishing a budget that is reasonable and then boldly raising support until we are fully funded.

Some missionaries hesitate to fundraise for a full budget. And some pastors hesitate to ask for a much-needed raise. Don't say your income is "fine," if it is not.

Many missionaries receive good pay, but how about you?

* Is your salary adequate? (Does your spouse agree?)
* Are you paying down debt?
* Do you save each month?
* Are you experiencing financial freedom? Or barely making it?
* How much stress are you feeling about financial matters?

If you had adequate pay, how would your ministry be better? How would your home life be better? Would adequate pay enable you to better advance the gospel?

1 Timothy 5:17–18

Day 22

PRAYER

Father of all, I didn't go into ministry to become wealthy, but I have been poorly funded for so long, it feels like "barely making it" is normal. I don't think I am being greedy. What changes should I make in my mindset and in my fundraising efforts? Show me that you've gone before me. Lead me. Amen.

23

FUNDRAISING PROCRASTINATION

But they all alike began to make excuses... None of those men who were invited shall taste of my dinner.

LUKE 14:18a, 24

In fundraising, it's easy to *make excuses*, to put it off until tomorrow or next week or never. Instead of setting a presentation appointment, we substitute filler activities — dreadful tasks like weeding the garden or alphabetizing the spice cabinet.

In our text today, Jesus told about a man who invited friends to a "big dinner" (Luke 14:16). But the friends made excuses for why they couldn't come. One bought a piece of land and needed to go look at it. Another needed to try out a new team of oxen, and a third had just gotten married. Sorry.

Their explanations seemed reasonable to them. But Jesus called them *excuses.*

And so it is in funding. Gospel workers often substitute filler activities for somewhat logical reasons. Who would criticize you for praying with a friend or reading to your child instead of working on fundraising?

But in our hearts, we know that we gave ourselves permission to substitute something pleasant for something distasteful. Procrastination is more about emotions than it is about time management.

Why do we procrastinate? Some common reasons:

* Fear of failure or rejection.
* Lack of skills. Not confident in what to do or how to start.
* Perfectionism. Unrealistically high standards make us stall even more.
* Vague or non-serious deadlines promote a lackadaisical attitude.
* Distractions. Disorder.

Let's consider procrastination from God's perspective — a sin. Are you serious? A sin?

Yes. For example:

A gospel worker believes it is God's will for him to work on fundraising this afternoon starting at two p.m. No emergencies are likely, the afternoon schedule is clear, he has a list of prospective partners to call, he knows what to do, and he knows how to do it.

Two p.m. arrives. He prioritizes his list. Suddenly his phone buzzes with an alert. He checks it. Nothing important, but while there, he decides to check Facebook. Twenty minutes pass. Then he checks LinkedIn "just for a few minutes." Next, an old friend calls "just to chat."

Then he needs coffee.

After coffee, he remembers the message on King David he is preparing for church in six weeks, so he decides to study a commentary on David's enemies, the Philistines.

Now two hours have passed. The kids arrive home from school. "Hey, dad!"

Fundraising is postponed. Couldn't be helped.

What happened here? When we sense God is leading us to work on fundraising but postpone it for no good reason, it is called procrastination. It doesn't just happen; it *is* a decision. In doing so, we give ourselves permission to walk away from God's leading.

Furthermore, procrastination is not merely a harmless bad habit. Researchers find that chronic procrastination contributes to low self-confidence and depression.

More importantly, in our text, Jesus warned that excuse-makers would not *taste* the Lord's dinner. Not tasting the Lord's dinner is a big miss!

Delayed obedience is disobedience. We can't call it anything else.

How about you? If you know what to do, why do you procrastinate? What are you trying to avoid?

I hastened and did not delay to keep your commandments.

PSALM 119:60

PRAYER

Lord of the Universe, I have never considered that procrastination could be a sin, nor have I ever asked myself why I procrastinate. Help me to be so in tune with the Holy Spirit that I do not indulge in feel-good activities instead of doing what I know is right. Amen.

24

SECRETLY WANT TO BE RICH?

But those who want to get rich fall into temptation and a snare and many foolish and harmful desires which plunge men into ruin and destruction. For the love of money is a root of all sorts of evil, and some by longing for it have wandered away from the faith and pierced themselves with many griefs.

1 TIMOTHY 6:9–10

At first glance, it seems like Paul is talking to wealthy people. Does our text also apply to missionaries? Paul doesn't say "those who *are* rich"; he says those who *want to get rich*. Wealthy people are often oblivious to their millions. And mission workers can be obsessed with money. You don't have to *be* rich to *want* to be rich.

It's important to note that nowhere does Jesus condemn the rich for being rich. Possessing wealth is not the problem. *Longing for it* is the problem. And it leads to big trouble, as we shall see.

Let's understand three things about this passage.

1 *It is written to Christians.* The phrase "wandered away from the faith" is the tip-off. A non-believer has no faith to wander from. Believers are not immune from wanting to be rich.

2 *Money is not the problem.* Verse 10 is perhaps the most misquoted verse in the Bible because it deletes one important word. Money is not a root of evil. *Love of money* is a root of evil.

   No missionary or Christian leader would say they love money. But if you are below budget, what occupies your (or your spouse's) mind? What do you think about every day?

   Below-budget missionaries are tempted to envy colleagues who are fully funded and living with margin. They might even envy a wealthy donor who has "nice things" and goes on "nice trips."

   A missionary friend who was well below budget criticized his fellow staff for making fundraising appeals which he considered unspiritual. Then he paused and said, "But I think about money all the time." An honest man!

3 *We don't bolt — we wander.* "Those who want to get rich" don't suddenly bolt from Christ — they *wander.* Slowly, they withdraw from fellowship with believers, they stop reading the Bible, and prayer seems mechanical.

   This is more serious than merely skipping church. Here is what awaits those who "wander from the faith": temptation, foolish and harmful desires, ruin, destruction, and piercing themselves with many griefs.

What seems like a harmless desire (wanting to be rich) ends with ruin and destruction.

Does working on your funding plan imply that you love money? No, not necessarily. You have a greater purpose: to advance the gospel with financial freedom.

Maybe you don't long for stacks of money lying around the house. More subtle is longing for what money can buy, e.g., flying first class or wearing designer clothing. Wanting to be rich is similar to wanting to be powerful or wanting to be noticed.

A caller to financial guru Dave Ramsey's radio show wanted to buy a fast-food franchise. He had good income, no debt, and his investments were growing. Ramsey commended him for being financially healthy.

Finally, Ramsey asked the caller *why* he wanted to buy a franchise. The caller answered, "To increase my income." Ramsey pressed, "Why? For what larger purpose?"

The caller had no other purpose; becoming wealthier was his only goal.

Billy Graham once said, "There is nothing wrong with men possessing riches. The wrong comes when riches possess men."

PRAYER

Creator of all, I find it easy to criticize secular people for wanting money, but I too am vulnerable. I don't think I long to be rich, but am I deceiving myself? Please speak to me about my heart's deepest values and tell me if I love money or if I'm wandering from the faith. Amen.

25

BEFORE YOU ASK:
#1 & #2 OF PAUL'S 4 P'S

I aspired to preach the gospel, not where Christ was already named... But as it is written, "They who had no news of Him shall see, and they who have not heard shall understand."

ROMANS 15:20–21

If you search the internet for "asking for charitable gifts," you will find tons of information about techniques of asking — active listening, alert body language, sensitivity to donors. Those are helpful tips.

Unfortunately, fundraising has become synonymous with asking only. But there is more to fundraising than simply asking. Asking must be preceded by Paul's first two "P's."

#1: PASSION

Our text says, Paul *aspired to preach the gospel.* Aspired is a strong word which means to earnestly strive. Paul does not casually share the gospel "now and then." He told the Corinthians, "Woe is me if I do not preach the gospel" (1 Corinthians 9:16).

Paul leads with his passion, not his financial need. People might give once or twice if you say, "Send money, I'll explain later," but they prefer to support projects about which they are inspired. They want more than merely bailing you out of a financial jam.

Notice that Paul states his passion in just ten words: *to preach the gospel where Christ was not already named.* By contrast, the following axiom in the high-tech world is true in missions also: *The more you know about a subject, the more difficult it is to communicate it to outsiders.*

Gospel workers often communicate to giving partners the same way they talk to their ministry teams. They use in-house lingo, TLA's (three-letter acronyms), and missiology terms. They are talking to themselves, unaware of their audience. It smacks of laziness.

Let us not assume we are dynamite communicators! Plan how you will communicate your passion in a way your audience will understand.

Now for classic Evangelical history about communicating vision: Former President of Navigators Lorne Sanny confessed to his wife Lucy that he sometimes struggled to explain his ministry passion. Navigators were in many diverse cultures, had many opportunities, and faced many unsolvable issues.

Lucy asked if he had days when the vision seemed clear. "Yes," he said, "some days it's crystal clear." Lucy replied, "On those days, *write it down.*"

That's good advice for all of us. Write it down! Study your mission purpose before you appeal to giving partners. Disentangle your thoughts in private.

In Luke 21:14 Jesus told the disciples *not to prepare beforehand*. However, that command is for the end times when arrested by authorities. In fundraising, you must prepare!

#2: PROMISE

What motivated Paul to preach the gospel? Interestingly, he doesn't mention his love for people or the nations, including Spain. Nor does he mention Christ's Great Commission.

Instead, he quotes from Isaiah 52:15. "They who had no news of Him shall see." Well acquainted with the Old Testament, this passage stuck in Paul's mind that the nations must have *news of Him!*

God's promise about the nations undergirded Paul's passion. We can imagine Paul quoting this promise to himself over and over. For me, I find wonderful encouragement by meditating on the promises God has given me, particularly during times of worry.

HOW ABOUT YOU?

1 *What's your passion?* Do you articulate it in a compelling way? Like Paul, can you boil it down to ten words?
2 *What's your promise?* What are one or two Scriptures that undergird your ministry calling?

Sharing your passion and promise sets the table for an appeal.

PRAYER

Lord Jesus, I find it easy to ramble about my vision. Help me to sort it out so I can articulate clearly while being sensitive to my listeners. And please undergird me with a Scriptural promise to give substance to my passion and to sustain me during tough times. Amen.

26

PROPEMPO:
#3 OF PAUL'S 4 P'S

Whenever I go to Spain — for I hope to see you in passing, and to be helped on my way there by you...

ROMANS 15:24a

Today's passage continues *Paul's 4 P's* of funding. Yesterday we looked at *Passion* and *Promise* — what to say *before* you ask. Paul didn't lead with his financial need. He first shared his ministry passion and promise (Isaiah 52:15).

But sharing your passion and promise alone is not enough to recruit giving partners. It is time for Paul's third P, *Propempo*.

#3: *PROPEMPO*

"Helped on my way" is the Greek word *propempo*, which

means "to send forward, assisting a person on a journey in supplying the requisites of a trip or accompanying him part of the way."

Two thousand years later, we misinterpret this phrase. We assume Paul was asking for moral support, prayers, and a send-off to Spain with Kenyan party samosas, ice cream, and a big hurrah. No. Paul was directly asking for financial assistance. That's why he used the word, *propempo*! It's a bold word, used nine times in the New Testament,[7] including Titus 3:13.

Diligently help [propempo] *Zenas the lawyer and Apollos on their way so that nothing is lacking for them.*

Nothing is lacking implies generously helping with physical needs.

Propempo has nothing to do with begging or hinting. All nine New Testament uses are unapologetically connected with advancing the gospel. 3 John 6 says, "Send [mission workers] on their way in a manner worthy of God."

Back to today. Ministry leaders often say, "I can boldly appeal for others, but not for my own support." That sounds humble and pious, but in our passage, Paul asked for his own support. His appeal was not about him. Getting to Spain with the gospel was the point.

If you struggle with asking others to support your ministry, you are allowing your emotions or your conscience to overrule your passion. You might not be as committed to your ministry as you think. Passion for ministry is measured not by your emotions as you pray, but by your forthrightness as you fundraise!

Like Paul, you have a *bold* passion for the Kingdom and a biblical *promise* undergirding it. Work to identify why are you timid in asking. Do you have a fear of offending? Are you stuck because two or three opinionated friends haunt your conscience? Does it feel too secular to have a slim margin of money in your bank account? Do you feel you are robbing others to enrich yourself?

If so, then something needs to change.

In his booklet *The Spirituality of Fundraising,* Henri Nouwen said, "As a form of ministry, fundraising is as spiritual as giving a sermon, entering a time of prayer, visiting the sick, or feeding the hungry."

You are right to reject the methods of fast-money hucksters. But you are not like that! You follow God's leading. You have a bold vision, and that vision requires bold asking. Biblical fundraising is a spiritual ministry. You can do it!

Looking back on my own appeals in ministry, if I could do it again, I would ask bigger and more boldly.

PRAYER

Father in Heaven, I have been conditioned by my conscience and my culture that it is sub-spiritual to "ask." But I wonder if I am making it too much about me. Holy Spirit, please speak deeply to my heart about why I struggle. You have given me a passion and a promise. By your grace, please help me to boldly invite others to advance your Kingdom. Amen.

27

BUILD PERSONAL RELATIONSHIPS: #4 OF PAUL'S 4 P'S

When I have first enjoyed your company for a while...

ROMANS 15:24b

Paul's first three P's — Passion, Promise, and *Propempo* (boldly asking) — work together to move you toward full funding. But without the fourth P, your success is only temporary. Busy as he was, Paul did not neglect *Personal Relationships* with giving partners.

#4: PERSONAL RELATIONSHIPS

Paul was eager to get to Spain with the gospel, but he lingered with the Romans, saying he wished to *enjoy your com-*

pany for a while. Verse 15:32 is similar: "Find refreshing rest in your company."

What did they talk about?

Romans 1:12 gives a clue. "That I may be encouraged together with you... each of us by the others' faith..." They shared their spiritual life with one another: they talked about Christ.

I have been asked by time-conscious missionaries if it is cost effective to spend time with donors without mentioning money. After all, we can't measure results from the hours spent with them. In fact, it costs money to be with them.

What would Paul say?

Paul's "donors" were not ATMs where you punch in your ID and cash pops out. Think about it. Do you go to the ATM for stimulating conversation? Do you ask about its welfare or how the family is doing?

My friend, Jeremie from the Ivory Coast, says, "I go to an ATM *only* when I need money!" Unfortunately, some mission workers treat their mailing lists like ATMs. They only communicate with them when they need money.

By contrast, Paul *enjoyed their company*! The Greek word means literally to be "filled up" with them. The Message says, "to enjoy a good visit with you."

Yet we resist taking time away from our focus ministry to spend time with giving partners. There seems to be an unspoken rule that 98 percent of our time must go to our ministry focus — campus, inner city, orphanage, whatever. That leaves only two percent of our time for fundraising and donor ministry.

Let's change the paradigm. Why not dedicate up to 20 percent of your time to fundraising and donor partner relationships, including cultivating non-donors? That's one day a week!

Impossible? Remember: If you neglect your donors today, you will spend much more than 20 percent of your time tomorrow struggling to recapture their support.

Also remember, unlike ATMs, every person on your mailing list has a beneath-the-surface story and it includes pain, uncertainty, and a desire to make a difference in their corner of the world.

During the first three months of the COVID-19 pandemic in 2020, I phoned 175 friends, donors, and acquaintances from our mailing list. I didn't know what to say. I simply asked, "How are you surviving?" No talk of money, just a listening ear and a prayer.

One giving partner was discouraged about their wayward child and said, "Scott, I am glad you phoned. I was hoping someone would call me *today*."

Slow down. Listen. Invite your partners to share their hearts. Be a safe place for them.

And continue the kindness even when they are not giving. A former giving partner told me, "When we had to stop giving because of employment problems, you continued to take an interest in us." Biblical fundraising is not merely about money. You are building a family of partners who care for you and your mission. Like Paul, make time to *enjoy their company*.

* How often do your giving partners hear from you? Be honest.
* What can you do to enrich their lives (spiritual or personal)?

PRAYER

Father of all, you have given me a passion for ministry, a promise from the Bible, and courage to propempo *boldly. Now please help me honor my personal relationships and future giving partners. Show me how I can minister to one of them today. Amen.*

28

FUNDRAISING AND SELF-ESTEEM

You wove me in my mother's womb. I will give thanks to You, for I am fearfully and wonderfully made...

PSALM 139:13–14a

What determines your self-esteem? Your appearance? Your accomplishments? Your IQ? People's opinions of you? *Your* opinion of you?

When you think about yourself, what words come to mind?

In 7th grade, I was standing at the water fountain in the gymnasium when my basketball coach hollered, "Hey sparrow legs!" Everybody laughed. I looked down at my legs and felt embarrassed. I laughed too, but ever since that moment, whenever I heard people in the gym snickering, I assumed they were snickering at me. I pulled up my socks to hide my tinker-toy legs.

Aren't we all haunted by unkind words from others?

Here are some examples I've heard:

* A father told his daughter, "You were a mistake. We never intended to have you."
* A young college grad was told by his boss that he "wasn't leadership material."
* A dad jokingly introduced his son to a visitor saying, "This is the dumb one."

Even spoken in jest, these words stick in our minds like burrs cling to socks when you hike off trail.

Do you find yourself mentally debating with the person who said those unkind words? He or she might not remember, but you do! Mental arguments with people from our past (dead or alive) drain our emotions and give that person control over us.

By contrast, perhaps your parents or teachers praised you for accomplishments which were not really accomplishments at all, like the participation trophy you received for losing in the first round of a soccer tournament. Psychologists now say that these superficial acknowledgments do not build self-esteem.

If your esteem is built on your looks, IQ, accomplishments in sports, performance in the classroom, or the positive critique from others, you are building your house on sand.

The world's advice on improving self-esteem includes physical exercise, listing your achievements, forgiving negative people, caring about your appearance, or mastering a new skill. These are helpful tips, but they don't address the core issue.

The core question should be: "What does God think of us?" Let us establish a new identity based on who God says we are. Our text today says we are *fearfully and wonderfully made*. And *you wove me in my mother's womb* — sparrow legs and all! And then the Psalmist gave thanks for the way he was made.

Here are more ways God thinks of you:

* You are His workmanship! (Ephesians 2:10)
* You are complete in Him! (Colossians 2:10)
* You are not condemned! (Romans 8:1)

Start seeing yourself from God's point of view. The Apostle Paul said in 1 Corinthians 4:3 that people's evaluations of him were "a very small thing." Then he added, "I do not even examine myself." Even Paul's opinion of Paul was not his source of self-esteem.

Furthermore, who says your opinion about yourself is accurate? Jeremiah 17:9 says, "The heart is deceitful above all things and desperately wicked."

Does self-esteem affect fundraising? Absolutely! Inaccurate self-esteem erodes your get-up-and-go. For example, if you cannot accept your physical body or feel you have a boring personality, you will be more likely to avoid risks, including the risk of asking for support.

But take heart, you can dive back into fundraising. Tonight, fall asleep thinking about how you are *fearfully made*, that you are *His workmanship*. Think about yourself the way God thinks about you. He loves how he made you, and you can too.

PRAYER

Father in Heaven, sometimes I don't like myself very much — my weight, my personality, my mannerisms. Plus, I can't forget those unkind words that I heard in the past. Please help me to think about myself the way you think about me. I choose today to say thank you that I am fearfully and wonderfully made. Amen.

29

CHECKING BACK WITHOUT OFFENDING

I give my opinion in this matter...[you] were the first to begin a year ago not only to do this, but also to desire to do it. But now finish doing it also, so that just as there was a readiness to desire it, so there may be also the completion of it by your ability.

2 CORINTHIANS 8:10–11

We've all experienced it. A potential giving partner indicates "yes" to monthly support. One month passes...two months pass...three months pass...and still no gift. You've left a voicemail, texted twice, and commented on their latest social media post. Are you becoming an unwelcome pest?

What did the Apostle Paul do in a similar situation? He

doesn't tell us how many times to call or text, but he does give us four important guidelines.

On his second and third missionary journeys, Paul had appealed to the new churches in Asia Minor and Greece to raise a "collection" for the suffering believers in Jerusalem.

And the Corinthians committed to support these fellow believers 700 miles east across the Mediterranean. They *were the first [church] to begin a year ago.* But would they follow through? So far, no gift.

So Paul sent Titus to Corinth to investigate (2 Corinthians 8:6), and Titus happily reported that the Corinthians intended to complete their giving. Paul was overjoyed and wrote his famous chapters on giving (2 Corinthians 8 and 9). Still, despite promising talk, money has not yet been given. Now Paul exhorts the Corinthians to finish what they started, to be "promise keepers," not merely "promise makers."

PAUL'S FOUR GUIDELINES:

1   *I give my opinion in this matter.* We are tempted to give up on promise makers — just let them go. But Paul courageously revisited the money subject: "You promised, what happened?"

In giving his *opinion*, Paul does not criticize nor demand. He doesn't even mention the "T" word (tithing). Like Paul, let us not be judgmental or demanding or promote "tithing guilt." Biblical giving is free will giving.

2   *Finish doing it.* Paul refers to the "high impulses" of the Corinthians, and he boldly exhorts them to finish because good intentions are not enough. Bible Commentator William Barclay said, "The tragedy of life so often is, not that we have no high impulses, but that we so often let them remain impulses and never turn them into actions." [8]

3 *By your ability.* Perhaps the Corinthians' financial conditions had changed since a year ago. If circumstances change, giving can change.

4 Teach biblical giving. Isn't money a private issue? Is Paul being too pushy? Why is he so insistent about the Corinthians following through?

Paul wants to help the suffering saints in Jerusalem. But he also wants to help the Corinthians integrate giving as a "basic" in their new Christian lives. Therefore, he devotes chapters 8 and 9 to *teaching* about giving. That's 39 verses!

Giving is part of discipleship; it's not optional. Let us boldly teach biblical giving to our people. That is why I quote and discuss 2 Corinthians 9:7 as I close my funding appeals: "God loves a cheerful giver."

Sess, a gospel leader in Francophone West Africa, offers to do a Bible study on giving with his "promise-making" friends. And he follows Paul's guidelines in saying:

I know you want to support us, but let's cancel what you originally promised and start over. What giving amount seems manageable for you now? I want to help you be a faithful biblical giver.

What can you do to teach biblical giving to your friends, family, and ministry contacts?

PRAYER

Father in Heaven, I hesitate to check back with my promise makers for fear of offending, but I must be fully funded to accomplish the calling you have given me. More importantly, help me follow Paul's example to enable my people to become faithful biblical givers. Amen.

30

IS 100% ABSOLUTELY NECESSARY?

Make it your ambition to lead a quiet life and attend to your own business and work with your hands, just as we commanded you, so that you will behave properly toward outsiders and not be in any need.

1 THESSALONIANS 4:11–12

As they begin, gospel workers experience an initial rush of fundraising success. They even receive gifts from "non-interested" acquaintances. Wow!

But soon, the "yeses" slow down. Weeks drag into months with meager results. With their funding deadline approaching, they wonder, "100 percent? Really? Surely I can get by on a lower budget!"

Veteran missionaries face the same dilemma. Sadly, many

lower their budgets, and sadly, their supervisors permit it. Soon they are short of cash, and their fundraising tactics become desperate. Or they determine to get by on 60 or 80 percent of their budget. The pain of getting by is less than the pain of fundraising, they conclude.

Our verse today admonishes believers to be attentive to their personal economics — that includes missionaries! Two phrases to notice:

"ATTEND TO YOUR OWN BUSINESS"

In both Thessalonian letters, Paul emphasized the imminent return of Christ, but it was mis-applied: "If Christ is coming back soon, why work?"

Some new Thessalonian believers were "leading an un-disciplined life, doing no work at all" (2 Thessalonians 3:11). Conveniently, Greek culture did not highly regard manual labor; it was fit only for slaves.

Were those Thessalonians who idled away their days waiting for the Lord's return "good Christians?" In a way, perhaps. They were certainly spiritually-minded Christians, but they neglected personal financial responsibility. Paul was also spiritually minded, but he went against the culture and championed hard work.

Followers of Christ cannot excuse financial irresponsibility in favor of lofty, super spirituality.

"SO THAT"

Whenever you see "so that" in Scripture, look for what comes next. Attend to your business *so that* you will:

* *Behave properly toward outsiders [non-believers].* Before joining the ministry, I worked in the advertising department at a newspaper in Missouri. A colleague who admitted he disdained Christians was watching me lay out a full-page ad on a large counter. But I

couldn't get the artwork to fit and was tight against my deadline. Under my breath I muttered, "Rats!"

My colleague stopped, took the cigarette out of his mouth and stared at me. Finally he asked, "What did you say?" "Ahh…Rats," I repeated.

"Whew!" He breathed a sigh of relief. "I thought you cussed!"

I was being watched! And you are being watched too!

* *Not be in any need.* Paul wanted the Thessalonica believers to be financially solvent, not financially "needy." In the early church, believers cared for the poor and started hospitals around the Mediterranean. They couldn't have been that generous without adequate personal cash flow.

   Years ago, I visited a city which was home to a mission agency. Many of the mission staff received government food stamps. Their reputation in the city was: "Always needy!"

As a missionary, do Paul's words apply to you? Yes! *Attending to your own business* means working hard at fundraising.

Give your mission agency the benefit of the doubt. If they say you need to be 100 percent funded, go for it. Missionaries who raise less than 100 percent are under constant financial pressure (young families feel it the most), they cannot save, and they are tempted by funding schemes.

It's not merely about money. Your financial testimony affects the advance of the gospel. Your extended family, former colleagues, neighbors — they are all watching!

PRAYER

Father of all, I confess I sometimes succumb to a "get-by" mentality.

Please give me the grace to attend to my business, not stopping until I am fully funded. May my finances enable me to behave properly toward outsiders. Amen.

Day 30

31

WHAT JESUS TAUGHT ABOUT TITHING

Woe to you, scribes and Pharisees, hypocrites! For you tithe mint and dill and cumin, and have neglected the weightier provisions of the law: justice and mercy and faithfulness; but these are the things you should have done without neglecting the others. You blind guides, who strain out a gnat and swallow a camel!

MATTHEW 23:23-24

If you asked the people on your mailing list how much Christians should give to the Lord's work, what would they say?

* 10%—tithe
* 10%—tithe to my local church, then additional offerings to missions
* 23 and 1/3% — the Bible mentions three tithes

* No more than you can give cheerfully — 2 Corinthians 9:7 (God loves a cheerful giver)
* "Give 'til it hurts, man!" —USA Hippies, 1965
* No rules — you decide
* Only when you feel you have extra
* Other

Around the world, most responses would focus on tithing. Tithe means literally "tenth," but many believers equate it with giving in general, which is not accurate. Of the forty times tithing is mentioned in the Bible, thirty-two are from the Old Testament, including the often-preached Malachi 3:10, "Bring the whole tithe into the storehouse..."

What did Jesus teach about tithing?

He mentioned it only twice. First, in Luke 18:11–14 Jesus described a Pharisee pridefully thanking God he was better than others, "I fast twice a week; I pay *tithes* on all that I get." Nearby, a tax collector prayed, "God, be merciful to me, the sinner!" This parable teaches humility, not tithing.

Second is today's text. Jesus does not criticize the Pharisees for *failing* to tithe — they were over-achievers in tithing. The Old Testament called for tithes only on grain, new wine, oil, and firstborn livestock (Deuteronomy 14:23). The Pharisees added garden plants (mint, dill, and cumin). Meticulous to a fault.

Jesus criticized them for neglecting the *weightier provisions of the law: justice, mercy, and faithfulness.* They majored on a minor. He exhorted them to focus on justice, mercy, and faithfulness "without neglecting the *others*."

Others is plural, referring to *other* Old Testament laws. Jesus expected Jews to be "good Jews," to follow their historic faith, including tithing.

What about Christ followers today? If we bring Old Testament tithing into the New Covenant, must we also bring other specific Jewish laws, such as dietary rules or circumcision?

Some teachers equate Malachi's "storehouse" (Malachi 3:10) with today's "church-house." That is a stretch. The storehouse was a granary built beside the temple to store excess grain during the reign of Hezekiah 250 years before Malachi.

The Apostle Paul was a Pharisee before his conversion — certainly a legalistic tither. Though Paul boldly taught generous giving, he is silent on tithing. Not a peep. His silence cannot be ignored. As a Christian leader, you are free to exhort believers to tithe, but you are *not* free to teach that Jesus or the New Testament endorsed tithing!

Back to our question: how much should Christians give? Start with Luke 21:1–4 where Jesus watched the rich putting their gifts into the treasury while a poor widow gave two coins. Jesus said she "put in more than all of them."

We should also study 2 Corinthians 8–9. And, if you are looking for a loophole to avoid giving generously to the local church, you will not find it (Galatians 6:6–10, 1 Timothy 5:17–18).

Teach your donors and future donors that the New Testament does not mandate a percentage for giving. They are free! And being free will likely cause them to give joyfully ("no rules!") and sacrificially ("'til it hurts, man!").

PRAYER

Father of all, as a missionary, sometimes I feel I "have to tithe" as a model for others. And sometimes, like the Pharisees, I feel prideful about my giving. May I be generous and sacrificial and model that for others. Thank you for freedom in giving. Amen.

32

PERFECTIONISM AND FUNDRAISING

He who watches the wind will not sow and he who looks at the clouds will not reap.

ECCLESIASTES 11:4

Our text today describes a farmer looking at the sky; watching the wind and looking at the clouds. Is it too windy to sow? It looks like rain, maybe I should wait.

In olden days, farmers sowed by hand, carrying a bag of seed and scattering it as evenly as possible. It wasn't easy. I was sowing grass seed on bare spots in our lawn a few years ago, but it was a windy day, and seeds flew everywhere! I should have waited until the next day.

Likewise, at harvest time, a farmer could say, "I cannot harvest today because it might rain." But if he delays too long, an October snowstorm could destroy his crop. Whizzing along Interstate Highway 80 in Midwest America during February, we often see un-harvested cornstalks buried in three-foot snowdrifts.

In farming, the weather is never perfect for sowing nor reaping. It is similar in fundraising: there's never a perfect time for asking, nor even for adding someone to your mailing list. Both farmers and fundraisers deal with a myriad of factors that are out of their control, yet they must take risks in order to make it.

Perfectionistic fundraisers prefer to wait and wait. It's like a bow hunter who says, "Ready... aim. Ready... aim," but never lets the arrow fly.

However, perfectionists get a bad rap. There's no denying that they have high ambition, they work hard, they're thorough, and they don't settle for mediocrity. For example, I want my surgeon to be a perfectionist!

In the right situation, perfection is necessary, but sometimes it hinders progress. In my 20s I worked for a cement contractor. One hot afternoon he watched me floating out a small sidewalk section of freshly laid cement. Trowel in hand, I smoothed the cement over and over to get it perfectly even. That's when he impatiently said, "Move on, Scott. We're making a sidewalk, not a watch."

But Jesus said, "Therefore, you are to be *perfect,* as your Heavenly father is perfect" (Matthew 5:48). The Greek word for perfect is *teleios* and means "complete or mature." It does not imply flawless perfection nor the arrogance that often goes with it. It's more like adult versus child.

In Matthew 5:44, Jesus said, "Love your enemies and pray for those who persecute you." It is in this context of relationships that He says, "*Therefore,* be perfect." We are to aspire to the maturity that loves people the way Christ loves them.

By contrast, aiming for flawless perfection is self-defeating and, if unchecked, causes "paralysis of analysis," the inability to make decisions. That leads to missing deadlines and failing to seize opportunities.

And so it goes in fundraising. It is better to make an 80-percent-okay presentation than to sit at your computer trying to make your graphics absolutely perfect.

On a crowded airplane, a mission leader, Gabe, was watching his younger colleague Bob share the gospel with his seatmate across the aisle. Bob was stumbling with his words and not giving his seatmate opportunities to ask questions. Gabe planned to give Bob some helpful critique after the flight.

But as Gabe got off the plane, it struck him that he never even thought of sharing the gospel with his seatmate. Bob's way of sharing the gospel was much better than Gabe's way of *not* sharing!

If you are drawn to (or paralyzed by) perfectionism, set a different goal: excellence. It means doing the best you can with the time, energy, and resources available to you right now. And it might be less than perfect.

Do your work heartily as for the Lord rather than for men.
COLOSSIANS 3:14

PRAYER

Father in Heaven, please help me avoid obsessing on perfection — especially in fundraising. Help me to "go as I am" rather than over preparing. Instead of perfectionism, may I work with excellence to honor you. Amen.

33

MINISTRY FATIGUE

Come to Me, all who are weary and heavy laden, and I will give you rest. Take My yoke upon you and learn from Me, for I am gentle and humble in heart, and you will find rest for your souls. For My yoke is easy and My burden is light.

MATTHEW 11:28–30

Over the years, I have heard weary gospel workers say, "If I could just take a couple weeks off…" But that's not possible, so they say, "If only I had a couple days to relax." But neither is that possible, so they finally say, "If I just had a couple hours to go off the grid…"

I have felt that way, and many people in other professions feel this way as well. It's hard to unplug! As gospel workers, we are conscientious. Our ministry work bleeds into our personal lives, and we feel like it is never done. And then there's fundraising!

Jesus understands our weariness. That's why He gives three invitations and a promise.

COME TO ME

Jesus beckons *all*. But to *come,* you must leave where you are. Consider those words one more time…To come, you must leave where you are. You are not coming to the Christian religion or to an organization or to ministry techniques. You are coming to a person. Jesus doesn't give formulas, He gives His *presence*.

When your soul is weary, stop. Put down your phone, get up from your desk — and *come*. John 7:37b says, "If anyone is thirsty, let him *come* to Me and drink." Sitting in Jesus' presence will calm you and give you His perspective on whatever you face.

YOKE WITH ME

This is a strange way of getting rest. A yoke is an instrument for work. Surely the weary need a warm bed or a vacation at the seashore! Work gives rest?

In verse 30, Jesus says his *yoke is easy*. The Greek word for easy means "fit for use" or "kindly" as opposed to hard or bitter.

William Barclay described yoke-making in ancient Palestine. After the ox was measured, "The yoke was then roughed out and the ox was brought back to have the yoke tried on…[and] adjusted so that it would fit well and not gall the neck of the patient beast." [9]

Perhaps above Jesus' carpentry shop was a sign declaring, "My yokes fit well."

Bearing a yoke by yourself is wearisome. Rest comes by laying aside your single yoke and slipping into the harness with Jesus. His yoke will fit you perfectly.

LEARN FROM ME

Farmers of yesteryear wisely yoked a younger ox with an experienced one. The untrained ox would kick at the reins and strain to have its own way to no avail. Soon the youngster learned to cooperate with the experienced yokemate.

When we take Jesus' yoke upon us, He patiently puts up with our kicking and straining, and soon we learn to pull in stride with Him and the *burden is light*. 1 John 5:3 says, "His commandments are not burdensome."

In our daily devotions, we often search for principles of ministry or solutions to difficult issues. But let us go simply to learn from Jesus. No agenda. *Seek Him* in your quiet times.

THE PROMISE

"You will find rest for your *souls*," not physical rest. Jesus didn't say, "I will give you a relaxing hobby." Physical rest is necessary, but if your soul is not at rest, even two weeks in the Bahamas will not satisfy.

Are you tired? Does fundraising seem harder than it actually is? Are you taking yourself too seriously? Are you constantly driven to "get it right?" Has ministry become joyless?

Jesus' promise is for you … today!

PRAYER

Lord Jesus, I am tired. Even energy drinks won't solve this problem. Fundraising especially fatigues me. I now come to you with a sincere plea. I put aside my yoke. I trust that your yoke will fit me well. May I experience your promise of rest for my soul. Amen.

34

ARE YOU BECOMING MORE LIKE CHRIST?

But we all, with unveiled face, beholding as in a mirror the glory of the Lord, are being transformed into the same image from glory to glory, just as from the Lord, the Spirit.

2 CORINTHIANS 3:18

When your giving partners look at you, what do you want them to see?

* Gifted, productive leader? (a good investment)
* Humble, but bold mission worker?
* Successful young man or woman with lots of potential?
* Cool Christian?

Or do you want them to see *Christ* in you?

Today's text gives two refreshing insights about becoming Christlike.

1   *Being transformed.* Christlikeness is not something we write on a do-list to be accomplished by week's end. Transformation is passive. It is done quietly by the Holy Spirit — *to* you or *for* you, not *by* you.

The Greek word is *metamorphe*—metamorphosis. Imagine a dead-looking grayish chrysalis unfolding into a colorful butterfly spreading its wings. In a similar way, the Spirit morphs us into Christ's image.

As young believers, a friend and I participated with twenty others in a week-long Christian discipleship road trip. At the end of day one, we were convicted about how self-centered we acted, especially how we talked mostly about ourselves. For day two, we decided to work at becoming more focused on others and what the Lord had for us to learn the rest of the week. We wanted to be more holy.

At the end of day two, we compared notes. Instead of improving, we were worse! Our thoughts were on ourselves constantly, particularly about how holy or unholy we acted. We were also far too focused on the behavior (and shortcomings) of others. In short, focusing on becoming holy produced a judgmental spirit.

2   *Beholding, as in a mirror, the glory of the Lord.* Mirrors in New Testament days were actually polished metal — not as clear as today's mirrors. The Holy Spirit does the transforming, but here is our role: to look carefully (as in an ancient mirror) to see not ourselves, but Jesus.

It is an axiom that we become like those we gaze upon. Youngsters often fixate on a music idol or a sports star and soon dress, talk, and act like their idol. In the 1990s Chicago Bulls basketball superstar Michael Jordan was as easily recognized as Mickey

Mouse. Many of us remember a popular commercial featuring kids singing, "I want to be like Mike!"

Missionaries can also put their eyes on the wrong object. E. Stanley Jones (1884–1973), a Methodist missionary to India, was considered the Billy Graham of India. Naturally, Jones was grateful to the man who led him to Christ, Robert J. Bateman, a powerful evangelist with a deep commanding voice. As a young gospel worker, Stanley began trying to mimic Bateman's rough speaking voice. In Jones' own words:

Jesus said to me one day, "[Stanley], are you following Robert J. Bateman or are you following Me?" I halted and said, "Why, Lord, of course, I am following You." Thereafter I would glance at men but gaze at Jesus.[10]

As wonderful as your heroes are, they did not die on the cross for you. Glance at people. Gaze at Jesus. To grow in Christlikeness, get your eyes off people, and get your eyes off yourself.

How about you? At whom are you glancing? At whom are you gazing? Whom do you want to be like? The best thing you can do for your giving partners is give them a glimpse of Jesus in you!

PRAYER

Father in Heaven, it's true, I get nothing but a judgmental spirit when I focus on "becoming holy." Instead of gazing at Christ, my eyes are often on _____ and _____. May your Holy Spirit transform me into your likeness. Amen.

35

WHY LITTLE THINGS MATTER

He who is faithful in a very little thing is faithful also in much, and he who is unrighteous in a very little thing is unrighteous also in much.

LUKE 16:10

Little things are those behind-the-scenes, small actions that advance your ministry. No one notices, not even your ministry supervisor. *Little things* are as silent as a cat staring at a bird feeder. They go unnoticed, especially in fundraising.

D.L. Moody, evangelist and founder of Moody Bible Institute said, "Many of us are willing to do great things for the Lord, but few of us are willing to do little things."

Our text today highlights not merely little things, but *very* little things. One who is faithful in a *very little thing* will be *faithful also in much*: in a big thing. If you do little things faithfully, chances are you will do big things faithfully. It's a spiritual discipline.

But if you are *unrighteous in a very little thing*, chances are you will be unrighteous in bigger things. This is serious.

When it comes to fundraising, we long to "get it over and done with." We daydream about a big donor who voluntarily gives spectacular gifts, freeing us from the time-consuming details of fundraising with many smaller donors.

But it rarely works that way. Missionaries who are fully funded usually have a wide base of partners, not one big benefactor. They take time to do little things to recruit many partners and to faithfully minister to them.

Here are eight fundraising little things. If you are doing some or all of these, good job!

1 Proofread your newsletter at least *three times* before you send. Your readers won't compliment you for accurate spelling, but they will notice misspellings.

2 Keep your mailing list data accurate. This is called "data hygiene." An up-to-date mailing list saves angst later when letters bounce back or you call a disconnected phone.

3 Personally thank a new donor within forty-eight hours from the time you hear of their gift. Similarly, be quick to thank a lapsed donor who restarts.

4 Rehearse exactly what you will say for your fundraising "ask." Don't force your donor to watch you painfully scramble (and ramble) for words.

5 Send an immediate thank-you note (an actual note in snail mail if possible) after staying in a donor's home overnight.

6 Fill out your Up 'Till Now Report twice a year to understand your fundraising status. This gives ideas for the next phase of funding and helps you follow up on "undecideds."

7 Phone monthly partners who skip two months con-
   secutively. Ask, "Is everything okay?"
8 Pray. Hardly a little thing, but it is behind the scenes.
   Bring your budget before the Lord daily—the exact
   amount. That's your "daily bread." Jesus told us to ask,
   after all!

Want to be fully funded? Faithfully do *little things* day by
day, week by week. No one will applaud you, but you will
have the privilege of advancing the gospel without finances
holding you back. Little things do matter!

For who has despised the day of small things?
ZECHARIAH 4:10A

PRAYER:

Father, where shall I work today?
And my love flowed warm and free.
Then He pointed out a tiny spot,
And said, "Tend that for Me."
I answered quickly, "Oh no, not that,
Why, no one will ever see,
No matter how well my work was done,
Not that little place for me!"
And the word He spoke, it was not stern,
He answered me tenderly,
"Ah little one, search that heart of thine;
Art thou working for them or Me?
Nazareth was a little place,
And so was Galilee."

—*Meade McGuire, Adventist Pastor (1875–1967)*

36

FUNDRAISING OR EVANGELISM?

And whatever city or village you enter, inquire who is worthy in it, and stay at his house until you leave that city...
He who receives you receives me, and he who receives me receives Him who sent me.

MATTHEW 10:11 & 40

Biblical fundraising requires giving special attention to the words: Inquire, Stay, Receive.

INQUIRE

Jesus had just finished instructing the Twelve on their first missionary journey to villages in Israel, to fellow Jews. They were not to take a money belt nor provisions. Go as you are, they were told!

Today, we would pre-arrange housing, pack a pillow, and a bag of our favorite snack. But Jesus did not permit that sort of planning this time. According to custom, fellow Jews were to show hospitality to traveling rabbis. But it was still a step of faith.

Upon entering a town, they were to inquire where to stay. The Greek word is *exetasate*, "to search diligently." In the Christmas story, King Herod used this word when he instructed the Magi to "search carefully for the Child" (Matthew 2:8).

Exetasate is your word when you run out of contacts, when the Holy Spirit nudges you to think outside the box. Stretch your mind, search diligently!

STAY

The disciples were to stay at the host's house until they left town. Wouldn't moving around town advertise their message more? Maybe, but staying with one host enabled them to deepen relationships with the entire household (*oikos*), meaning extended family, servants, *and* their friends.

This is a good reminder to deepen relationships with potential giving partners, even if they know little about your ministry. Did those who hosted the Twelve understand Jesus' ministry in the beginning?

RECEIVE

Here is a dramatic promise. "He who *receives* you receives Me, and he who receives Me receives Him who sent Me!" Receive is the Greek word *dechomai*, and means "to welcome."

In welcoming you, your potential donors are welcoming Jesus and the One who sent Jesus. You are not only fundraising, but you are also bringing the God of the universe to potential donors!

This is why I always share my journey to Christ. For example, during supper at a fundraising appointment with

Jerry and Marge, whom we had recently met, we shared our spiritual journeys. Our testimonies were well-received; they seemed to enjoy what we shared.

Then Marge said to her husband Jerry, "Tell them your testimony, honey!" Looking sheepish and clearing his throat, Jerry finally said, "I got nothing."

Marge nudged him in a not-so-subtle way and said, "Jerry, you prayed the prayer!"

"Yeah," Jerry said sarcastically, "I prayed the prayer!"

Awkward! A few seconds passed though it seemed like a few minutes. It was then that I knew we should keep our fundraising appeal off the table. So I asked Jerry if he would like to meet for Bible study so we could both learn more about Jesus.

Jerry said, "You wouldn't want to meet with a sinner like me!"

I replied, "I'm a sinner too, Jerry." And we set a bi-weekly meeting time.

Now it's your turn. Think about a recent fundraising appointment. Was it in a home, on Zoom, or at a restaurant? Did you realize that Jesus was sitting right there with you? If your listeners welcomed you, they also welcomed Jesus and the One who sent Jesus.

This takes fundraising out of the realm of the secular. Your fundraising appointments are holy times of advancing the gospel. Don't forget to tell your story!

PRAYER

Father in Heaven, who are the worthy hosts that you have prepared for me? Please help me to inquire, to take the risk of meeting new people, and to stay with them — building genuine friendships. May I remember that as my hosts receive me, they also receive you. Amen.

JOY IN FUNDRAISING TRIALS

Consider it all joy, my brethren, when you encounter various trials, knowing that the testing of your faith produces endurance. And let endurance have its perfect result, so that you may be perfect and complete, lacking in nothing.

JAMES 1:2–4

If you have not yet experienced financial trials, don't worry, they are coming! Our text says *when* you encounter trials, not *if*. And among missionaries, financial trials are common.

Your financial trial might come when:

* You hear a "No," but it feels like "HECK NO!"
* Your car mechanic says he has both good news and bad news.

* Your donor report from headquarters is once again disappointing.
* You run out of fundraising contacts and don't know where to turn.

Even the godly prophet Elijah experienced funding trials. On the run from wicked Queen Jezebel, he drank from the brook Cherith. But 1 Kings 17:7 says, "It happened after a while that the brook dried up..."

Our passage today is a classic Scripture on trials of all kinds. Three words stand out:

1 *It. Consider it all joy.* Did you know the word "it" is not in the earliest manuscripts? You needn't pretend that the trial is joyful, or that the cause of the trial is joyful. And don't think that you must "gut it out" either. Instead, because of Christ, "*consider joy*" as you go through the trial.

2 *Endurance.* In the old days of ship building, tall masts to hold the sails were not chosen from trees sheltered in the valley, but from trees in windy, stormy places on the mountains. Having endured buffeting storms, these trees made stronger masts.

   In similar fashion, financial trials give you an opportunity to develop endurance. Stormy winds make you stronger.

3 *Perfect.* Does this mean you can become perfect—never sinning again? No, the Greek word is *teleios*. It implies being "fit for a task," like an athlete who has completed his training and is now prepared to compete in the games.

   Through your trials, you become fit for opportunities God has uniquely prepared for you. Every difficulty you have faced in life up until now (though painful at the time) has equipped you to do what God has prepared for you today.

Isn't this what we want? To be fit to be what God has called us to be? And to be fit to do what He has called us to do? It's the hard times that develop our character the most, that burn into us the convictions we hold.

On July 30, 1967, an 18-year-old named Joni Erickson Tada dived into shallow water in Chesapeake Bay and was severely injured, becoming paralyzed from the shoulders down.

Understandably, she struggled as a quadriplegic with anger, depression, and suicidal thoughts. But finding strength in Christ, Joni didn't give up. With a brush clenched between her teeth, she became an artist. And then she went on to write over forty books. Joni has a worldwide ministry to those with disabilities called Joni and Friends. She has joy through trials indeed!

Gospel worker, whether your trials are financial disappointments, family dysfunction, ministry setbacks, or poor health, *consider joy*. Christlike maturity requires tribulation.

My mother frequently quoted this poem:

It is easy enough to be pleasant
When life goes by like a song,
But the man worth his while
Is the one who can smile,
When everything goes dead wrong

— *ELLA WHEELER WILCOX, AMERICAN AUTHOR AND POET*
(1850–1919)

PRAYER

Sovereign Lord, like Elijah, my brook has dried up, finances have me feeling down. Help me to steadfastly endure and not resent this trial.

You are the "blessed controller" of all things. The "it" is painful, but today I choose joy as I surrender to your guidance. Amen.

Day 37

James 1:2–4

38

A PROMISE FOR YOUR FUNDING

Trust in the Lord with all your heart and do not lean on your own understanding. In all your ways acknowledge Him, and He will make your paths straight.

PROVERBS 3:5–6

What do you do when you don't know what to do next in fundraising? Should you ask Mr. Big Money Guy to increase to $10,000, hold a fundraising dinner, send an appeal letter, or focus on your end-of-year appeal in December?

Our text today is a classic discipleship passage. Let's look at it through the lens of funding.

DO NOT LEAN ON YOUR OWN UNDERSTANDING

It does not say *ignore* your own understanding. Psalm 32:9

agrees: "Do not be as the horse or as the mule which have no understanding…"

God gave you a mind — use it. Think hard to create a wise funding plan. Challenge yourself to write more articulate newsletters. Stretch your brain to describe a struggling new believer in your ministry. And in your appeals, honestly share your emotions, too.

But even on our sharpest days, human understanding is prone to error. It can cause us to believe lies about fundraising, such as "fundraising is begging" and "no one will support you in this economy. Get a real job!"

Also, human understanding prevents us from seeing the huge opportunities that God sees for us. Most missionaries have an unspoken "cap" on how much money they think they can raise. Double it! Triple it! His ways are far beyond our ways (Isaiah 55:8).

So, use your mind, seek understanding, but do not *rely* on your understanding. "He who trusts in his own heart is a fool" (Proverbs 28:26).

ALL YOUR HEART

Trusting God with all your heart means you may not sit on the fence — no "Plan B" in case God doesn't come through. If you stand with one foot on a rock and one foot in quicksand, you still sink.

"Plan B" for younger mission workers might be, "My parents will bail me out," or "My spouse's job will fund my work if necessary." For mid-career people, "Plan B" might include, "I'll get my old job back," or "I'll tap into my retirement funds."

As long as you cling to "Plan B," the Lord sits on the sidelines waiting. Is there a secret closet in your life to which the Lord does not have access? Is that where you keep "Plan B"?

ALL YOUR WAYS

Acknowledging God in *all your ways* means practicing the Presence of God, bringing every activity, every decision to the Lord moment by moment. We acknowledge God in big decisions, but what about small decisions, even small fund-raising decisions?

Acknowledging to the Lord each detail of your funding plan will calm you. And you will see Him in action! For example, pray before you:

* Appeal to Mr. Big Money Guy.
* Hit "send" on your newsletter.
* Phone "Bob and Cindy" to set an appointment.

I find that praying about small details gives me confidence that God's hand is on me. I am more relaxed around people, and things seem to go well — really well!

HE WILL MAKE YOUR PATHS STRAIGHT

The King James version says, "He shall direct thy paths." We serve a God who intervenes and directs us along straight paths. He does not stand aloof, watching us struggle. He dives into the fray with us! If your fundraising feels like a forest path that is becoming fainter the further you walk, stop and acknowledge Him. He *will* direct your path.

PRAYER

Thank you, Father, for being a God who guides. Today I am off the fence. I give you my "Plan B." I surrender to your plans for my funding. No longer will I lean on my own understanding. I count on you to direct my path. I want your plan, not my own. Amen.

39

YOUR BIBLE — THE INSPIRED WORD OF GOD

All Scripture is inspired by God...

2 TIMOTHY 3:16

Be honest. Do you, as a gospel worker, ever have doubts about the Bible? You are not alone, especially if the Bible is ridiculed by your family or friends.

One solution in dealing with Bible difficulties was made famous by U.S. President, Thomas Jefferson. In 1820, following his presidency Jefferson created his own Bible, known to history as the Jefferson Bible. Jefferson took a razor and cut out of the King James Bible all references referring to Jesus' miracles. Hmmm, interesting tactic.

By contrast, in our text today, Paul, the Old Testament

expert, says that *all* Scripture is inspired by God — not most, but ALL.

What about Jesus?

Jesus believed His Bible (the Old Testament) was accurate. For example, He taught about Jonah and the great fish (Matthew 12:40), the Creation of Adam and Eve (Matthew 19:4), and the destruction of Sodom and Gomorrah (Luke 17:28–29).

More than that, Jesus ordered his life around the guidance in the Bible.

* When tempted, He quoted Deuteronomy 8:3: "Man shall not live by bread alone" (Matthew 4:4).
* Jesus obeyed the Scriptures by traveling to Jerusalem to be crucified saying, "All things which are written through the prophets about the Son of Man will be accomplished" (Luke 18:32).

Two additional factors help me trust the Bible. First, the Bible doesn't candy-coat leadership mistakes. Most ancient literature praises its heroes, but ignores their sins. By contrast, the Bible details David's adultery with Bathsheba and Peter's three-time denial of Christ.

Second, geography and dates are specific, not "A long time ago in a galaxy far, far away." For example, in Luke 3:1, John the Baptist preached, "In the 15th year of the reign of Tiberius Caesar, when Pontius Pilate was governor of Judea, and Herod was Tetrarch of Galilee…" That's a lot of historical and geographical detail. Many times, names, places, and dates mentioned in the Bible are also found in secular records.

In 1949, as he began his ministry, evangelist Billy Graham struggled with the inerrancy of the Bible. How could he preach if the Bible was not reliable? In the words of his grandson, Will Graham:

One night at Forest Home [conference center in California]

[Billy] walked out into the woods and set his Bible on a stump...and he cried out: "O God! There are many things in this book I do not understand...There are many seeming contradictions...some [passages] do not seem to correlate with modern science..."

And then, my grandfather fell to his knees and the Holy Spirit moved in him as he said, "Father, I am going to accept this as Thy Word — by faith! I'm going to allow faith to go beyond my intellectual questions and doubts, and I will believe this to be Your inspired Word!" [11]

A bridge had been crossed.

Speaking at the University of Iowa, theologian Kenneth Kantzer, former president of Trinity Seminary, said, "It is not the things I *don't* understand in the Bible that bother me. It's the things I *do* understand but find difficult to put into practice."

What does inerrancy have to do with fundraising? Plenty! If you second-guess the reliability of the Bible, you will not speak with authority. Your devotional life will dry up like a crispy sunburned leaf fallen from a tree. And you will come across as disingenuous in your fundraising.

God is not afraid of your questions. Work diligently to understand the Scriptures. For those passages you don't understand, remember that you are not the judge of their accuracy. Put your razor away and trust God's Word.

PRAYER

Father in Heaven, I don't understand some passages in the Bible. You put them there for a reason, so I choose to believe that every line of your book is accurate and reliable. I decide today to believe the Word with humility and teach it with confidence. May you empower me by your Holy Spirit. Amen.

40

COULD YOU BECOME A
LOVER OF MONEY?

*Now the Pharisees, who were lovers of money, were listening
to all these things and were scoffing at Him.*

LUKE 16:14

The spiritual leaders of Jesus' day had a three-word reputation: *lovers of money*. And everyone knew it. Even Jesus said
the Pharisees "devoured widows' houses" (Matthew 23:14).

How did these serious Bible teachers become lovers of
money? And scoffers of Jesus!

Some background: Starting around 597 BC when the Jews
were forcibly deported from Israel to Babylon (present-day
Iraq), zealous scribes risked their lives to preserve the Old
Testament writings. Then, for 500 years, Israel was overrun
by Persians, Greeks, and finally in Jesus' day, Romans. These

scribes became the Pharisees, the "separated ones." They championed the law of Moses while Israel flirted with Babylonian, Persian, Greek, and Roman morality.

Let's give them credit. The 6,000 Pharisees of Jesus' day loved God, and they loved His Word.

But what went wrong? Did they suddenly go from loving God to loving money? More likely, they drifted little by little, similar to 1 Timothy 6:10. "Some by longing for [money] have *wandered* away from the faith..."

What about today? The news media howls when evangelical leaders are caught embezzling money or living extravagantly. It is well-documented that the unethical lifestyles of believers (especially in finances) have hindered the gospel.

What about you? You spend many hours in fundraising. You check your donor report often. You meticulously document ministry expenses. Could you become a lover of money?

Like the Pharisees, despite our love for the Lord and His word, we too could wander.

Love of money is actually a disguise for *love of power or love of pleasure.* We don't love $20 bills or Kenya Shillings or Japanese Yen per se, but we can love the things they buy. Money can surround you with shiny electronic gadgets, fly you first class, and take you to prestigious restaurants, all for ministry purposes, of course. Plus, wealth seems to prove to skeptical family and peers that you — the lowly Christian worker — have finally arrived.

As a former Pharisee, the Apostle Paul understood the lure of money. He said, "Those who *want to be rich* fall into temptation and a snare" (1 Timothy 6:9). Paul was not writing to money-hungry pagans, but to money-hungry Christians!

In like manner, the writer of Hebrews warned: "Make sure that your character is free from the *love of money*, being content with what you have; for He himself has said, 'I will never desert you, nor will I ever forsake you'" (Hebrews 13:5, quoting Deuteronomy 31:6).

Friends may forsake you, family may forsake you, and even your stock portfolio can fail you, but Christ will never forsake or fail you. Yes, you need money. But don't love money. Let us not worship the Almighty Dollar!

However, be careful. A love affair with money can also show up in worshiping frugality. Being overly preoccupied with or even bragging about living meagerly might reveal that money occupies first place in our minds.

Martin Luther famously said there are three conversions: head, heart, and wallet. Has your wallet been converted?

Albert was a Christian leader in Abuja, Nigeria. As a wealthy businessman, he too had a reputation, not as a *lover of money,* but as a *lover of people*. He regularly invited Christian ministries to use his home for meetings, and he provided their meals. When asked why he was so generous, Albert replied, "If God owns me, then He owns my pockets."

How about you? Does God own your pockets?

PRAYER

Lord Jesus Christ, owner of all, I confess that at times I am hungry for the things money can buy. Help me to see money for what it is: a medium of exchange and not the measure of my worth. May the phrase lover of money never apply to me. Amen.

BONUS: TEMPTED TO QUIT?

And His disciples answered Him, "Where will anyone be able to find enough bread here in this desolate place to satisfy these people?" And He was asking them, "How many loaves do you have?" And they said, "Seven."

MARK 8:4–5

In today's text we find Jesus outside His Jewish boundaries to teach in the primarily Gentile region of Decapolis — the ten cities — southeast of the Sea of Galilee. He went there by design — to the Gentiles!

After three days of teaching, Jesus felt compassion because the crowd had "nothing to eat." He hinted to His disciples that food was needed. Otherwise, the people will "faint on the way [home]" (Mark 8:2–3).

The disciples' response was pessimistic, but also realistic. Imagine the silence that followed when they asked, "*Where will anyone be able to find enough bread here in this desolate place to satisfy these people?*" The disciples didn't know what to do. Hopelessness crept down the hillside like dense fog.

You know the rest of the story. Jesus directed the people to sit down. That was risky because it raised the crowd's expectations. What if Jesus couldn't deliver? The disciples might not get their supper. Next, Jesus took the seven loaves, blessed them, and gave them to the amazed disciples who handed them out to the people. After everyone was fed, they picked up "seven large baskets" (Mark 8:8) of leftovers! What a miracle! Mind you, these baskets were not the small tote bags that Jews usually carried, but larger baskets, the type used to lower Paul over the wall in his escape from Damascus in 2 Corinthians 11:33.

When the disciples didn't know what to do, Jesus did. He knew their need before they did. Jesus' strategy? He started with what they had — seven loaves of barley bread and a "few small fish" (Mark 8:7).

What about you? Are you in a *desolate place,* not sure about what to do next? Some reading this feel ready to quit ministry altogether.

Listen to Jesus asking, "How many loaves do you have?" You might say, "I don't know any rich people." Fine, but you have something, you are not empty. Like Jesus, start there. Maybe you have a:

* Compelling vision for ministry — God's calling on your life
* Reputable organization
* Loving spouse
* Mailing list of 289
* Cell phone contacts list of 765 "friends"

List your "assets," and give them to Jesus. Ask Him for an idea. Let Him surprise you with seven baskets of leftovers.

God did this miracle long ago in Decapolis, a desolate

Gentile area that was outside the disciples' comfort zone. Can He do it again? Bible teacher A. W. Tozer said, "Unbelief says some other time, but not now; some other place, but not here; some other people, but not us."

In your country, is there no food? Among God's people, is there no bread? In your city, are there no like-minded people? In your cell phone, are there no generous hearts?

Why not now? Why not here? Why not you? Not sure what to do next? Give your seven loaves to Jesus and let Him multiply them to seven large baskets! It's not time to quit, not today!

PRAYER

Father of abundance, I often look at what I can't do rather than what You can do. I give You my seven loaves. Please multiply them according to your goodness. Help me to trust you according to Ephesians 3:20, "Beyond all that we could ask or think according to the power that works within us." Amen.

1   This and all Greek words researched in this book come from *Expository Dictionary of New Testament Words* by William Edwy Vine, published by Fleming H. Revell Company, 1966.

2   Manning, Brennan, *Abba's Child: The Cry of the Heart for Intimate Belonging.* Copyright 2015. Used by permission of NavPress, represented by Tyndale House Publishers, a Division of Tyndale House Ministries. All rights reserved.

3   Krejcir, Dr. Richard, "Statistics on Pastors," accessed August 8, 2021, www.intothyword.org.

4   Barclay, William, *The Daily Bible Study Series — Corinthians*, (Philadelphia: Westminster Press, 1956), 74.

5   Hogan, Chris, *Everyday Millionaires*, (Ramsey Press, Brentwood, Tennessee, 2019), 9.

6   Morton, Scott, *Down to Earth Discipling*, (Colorado Springs: NavPress, 2003), 9.

7   Acts 15:3, 20:38, 21:5, Romans 15:24, 1 Corinthians 16:6 and 11, 2 Corinthians 1:16, Titus 3:13, 3 John 6

8   Barclay, William, *The Daily Bible Study Series — Corinthians*, (Philadelphia: Westminster Press, 1956), 256.

9   Barclay, William, *The Daily Bible Study Series, The Gospel of Matthew, Volume 2*, (Philadelphia: Westminster Press, 1958), 17.

10   Jones, E. Stanley, *A Song of Ascents: A Spiritual Autobiography*, (Nashville: Abingdon Press, 1968), 37.

11   Quoting from story told by Will Graham, Access date, August 14, 2021, https://billygraham.org/story/will-graham-honors-his-grandfather-as-billy-graham-exhibit-opens-at-the-museum-of-the-bible/.

Scott Morton serves as International Funding Coach for The Navigators and frequently teaches on the topic of Biblical Fundraising and Stewardship. For twelve years, Scott served as U.S. Vice President of Development. Besides mentoring missionaries and leaders in funding, he enjoys helping skeptics grow in their spiritual journeys through small-group Bible studies and one-on-one mentoring of university students and businesspeople.

Scott is the author of seven books, including *Funding Your Ministry, Down to Earth Discipling, Blindspots,* and *What the Bible Actually Says about Money.* He and his wife live in Colorado Springs and have three children and four grandchildren. Scott's hobby is birding. Learn more at scottmorton.net.

What do you say to a friend who asks you, "God has called me to ministry, but first, I must raise personal support—what do I do?"

Sadly, many great ministries stop right here. But it need not be so. Refer your ministry friends to scottmorton.net to empower them with resources for their fundraising ministry.

THE WEBSITE INCLUDES:

130 three-minute videos on felt-need topics like:

* How to ask
* Who to invite for support
* How to minister to donors
* How to write newsletters that people will joyfully read
* Blogs with helpful lessons from international gospel workers
* Downloadable worksheets to help you plan your strategy
* Bible studies on what the Bible actually says about fundraising
* Q & A
* Spanish and French language tabs

Start with the International Bible Study on Fundraising. Mission workers around the world say the most helpful part of any fundraising training they receive is in this Bible study.

At last, a non-threatening resource for your giving partners in the touchy area of money!

Discipleship in finances is rarely talked about, because pastors are often criticized for speaking about money. Your people may never hear this content.

The Bible has over 2,000 verses on money, but let's start with 31 — day by day. That's doable! You can find how-to books on managing money, but this devotional speaks to the attitudes behind the how-to's — the heart behind our stewardship in this unspoken area of discipleship.

This devotional book is written for believers and non-believers alike. It does not focus on giving but on the entire spectrum of biblical stewardship. *Find it at scottmorton.net*

CHAPTER TITLES INCLUDE:

* How did Jesus fund His ministry?
* Eight Ways to go Broke
* Was Jesus Poor? Was Jesus Rich?
* The Secret of Saving
* Seven Financial Words to Pray Daily
* Supporting the Poor with Dignity

"Pastors often fear talking about money. Scott Morton uses the Bible's historical background to explode myths that strangle our freedom to talk about financial matters."

—**Pastor Randy Scheil**, Cedar Rapids, Iowa

"*What the Bible Actually Says About Money* gives biblical answers to the financial questions no one talks about. Scott Morton brings fresh insight to Scriptures you've read dozens of times but never considered in the context of money."

—**Leura Jones**, soccer mom trying to pay for college, French horn lessons, braces, summer camp, and new basketball shoes